Freedom and Discipline in English

Report of the Commission on English

College Entrance Examination Board
New York

Additional copies of this book may be ordered from College Entrance Examination Board, Publications Order Office, Box 592, Princeton, New Jersey 08540; or Box 1025, Berkeley, California 94701. The price is $2.75 for the clothbound edition and $1.75 for the paperbound edition.

Letters should be addressed to the Executive Director, Commission on English, 687 Boylston Street, Boston, Massachusetts 02116.

Members of the Commission on English

Harold C. Martin, Harvard University, *Chairman*

Floyd Rinker, *Executive Director*

Leslie L. Guster, *Assistant Director**

Frances D. Bartlett, Scarsdale, New York, High School

Verda Evans, Cleveland, Ohio, Public Schools

Arthur E. Jensen, Dartmouth College

Glenn Leggett, University of Washington

John A. Myers Jr., The Hun School, Princeton, New Jersey

Edward S. Noyes, College Entrance Examination Board, *ex officio*

Winifred L. Post, Dana Hall School, Wellesley, Massachusetts

Warner G. Rice, University of Michigan

David A. Robertson Jr., Barnard College

Louise M. Rosenblatt, New York University

Hallett D. Smith, California Institute of Technology

James R. Squire, University of Illinois

George Winchester Stone Jr., New York University

---

*1961-62, Robert F. Hogan
1962-63, Joseph W. McCloskey

Acknowledgments

The work of the Commission has been generously supported by the College Entrance Examination Board through successive allotments from its annual budgets. For operation of the original 20 Summer Institutes substantial grants were also received from The Bing Fund, Inc., The Danforth Foundation, Hobby Foundation, The Old Dominion Foundation, Victoria Foundation, Inc., and from Duke University and the New York State Department of Education. To all these sources of financial aid and moral support, members of the Commission wish to express their thanks. They are also grateful for continuing advice and encouragement from Frank Bowles and Richard Pearson, presidents of the Board during tenure of the Commission, and especially from Edward S. Noyes, vice-president of the Board, who has worked closely with the Commission in its deliberations.

The Commission accepts responsibility for the final form of this report but wishes to express its thanks for the help given by its own members, and for the special assistance of Arthur Carr, University of Michigan; Frederic Cassidy, University of Wisconsin; Scott Elledge, Cornell University; J. J. Lamberts, Arizona State College; and Albert H. Marckwardt, Princeton University.

Foreword

The publication of this report of the Commission on English is a source of genuine satisfaction to the member institutions, the trustees, and the officers of the College Entrance Examination Board. It is the culmination of five years of study, discussion, experimentation, and synthesis by the Commission and its staff. It presents what the Commission believes to be a consensus among teachers of English on the essential characteristics of the subject. Further, it presents ideas for the improvement of instruction in English. Actual improvement rests, as it must, upon the 100,000 teachers of English in the secondary schools throughout the country. The Commission's report is addressed to those teachers and to the administrators, school board members, and citizens who can and should support their efforts.

The report should be viewed as a part of the curricular reform that began in the early 1950's and has swept over the schools. It should take its place with comparable reports in other subjects, particularly in mathematics, the sciences, and foreign languages. We hope that the acceptance of the Commission's report will equal that given earlier reports in other fields, and that the response, in the form of effective changes in the classrooms, will be equally dramatic.

This may be too much to hope for. Restlessness about the quality of English instruction has existed among teachers of English for decades. It may be true that thoughtful English teachers have always been and always will be dissatisfied with their performance, because English, unlike other subjects, occupies a central position in the instructional program of the country's schools. The teaching of English aspires to no less than the intelligent use and understanding of language on the part of all students—in Robertson Davies' words, "Toward clarity of information in those subjects where information and deduction from language are the principal aims, and clarity of opinion in those subjects where personal opinion is of value."

The Commission was fully aware of the importance of this objective for the students who will be the future citizens of a great democracy. Its members are equally aware of the vast distance between the efforts they have made and the fulfillment of that objective. But it is time to start reducing the gap.

Although the Commission's tenure has expired, its work is far from over. Recognizing that the Boston office of the executive director has become a center for information and advice about all matters pertaining to the teaching of English, the trustees of the College Board voted in September 1964 to keep it in operation for at least three years. It was the trustees' hope that this action would constitute useful support to the United States Office of Education, and to the educational community generally, in connection with the National Defense Education Act and its recent extension to include English and reading.*

Francis Bacon wrote that "Reading maketh a full man, conference a ready man, and writing an exact man." We commend this report to all who believe that reading, speaking, and writing well are essential to the national welfare. We convey our respect and appreciation to the Commission on English, especially its chairman and executive director, for clarification of the issues and a plan for action.

Richard Pearson
President of the College Entrance Examination Board

---

*This hope has been fulfilled. There is ample evidence to show that the pioneer work of the Commission on English is proving exceptionally valuable, not only to the Office of Education, but also to colleges and universities planning to establish institutes under the amendments to NDEA. At the request of the Office of Education, and with the full cooperation of the College Board, the Modern Language Association has reprinted the Commission's documents about its institutes (see Appendix C of this report) and has made them widely available to institutions of higher learning. The Office of Education has also made use of individuals who had experience on the Commission or with its institutes, as consultants or as members of the task force to review proposals for the NDEA government-sponsored 1965 institutes. R.P.

Contents

The Quality of Instruction in English

What is English?

The Commission on English was appointed by the College Entrance Examination Board in September 1959. Broadly stated, the Commission's purpose was to improve the teaching of English in America's schools and colleges. It sought to encourage and facilitate a gradual nationwide improvement in curriculum, teacher training, and the methods of classroom instruction. Its stated goal was to propose standards of achievement for college preparatory students and to suggest ways of meeting them. The Commission's concern with college preparatory courses in secondary schools may seem to have been narrow, but experience with students in the College Board Advanced Placement Program continues to reveal that better teaching of able students affects the whole school. The Commission's efforts, then, though aimed at one group, are intended to influence all tracks and all levels.

In making this appointment, the Board reflected widespread concern that secondary school English, through a long process of diffusion, of trying to meet many needs not met elsewhere in the school, was in danger of losing its identity altogether. Someone's wry comment that English teaching is not a profession but a predicament seemed too close to the truth for comfort.

In the early elementary grades, where a single teacher commonly supervises all the child's studies and where attention span is short, the separate "subjects" are many. Lessons called history, geography, science, art, music, arithmetic take approximately half of the school day. The other half is given to reading, spelling, word study, penmanship, composition, oral work. In the later elementary years and thereafter, the second group is gradually compressed into a fifth of the school day and is merged into a single subject called "English." This compression has merit because it brings together several activities that have much in common, but it also has defects. In the first place, it makes separate what is naturally a part of other subjects: reading is part of history, spelling is part of science, word study is implicated everywhere, and so on. In the second place, exactly because the composite called "English," as it emerges from the elementary school, bears on all studies, it invites a further accumulation of responsibilities by the English teacher. At one pole, the study of logic may be added, though it is surely as much the province of geometry and physics as of English; at the other, social conduct (how to use the telephone, how to write letters of invitation, how to face teen-age problems) may claim time and attention. Whatever may be said about the absolute worth of some of these matters, it is clear that inclusiveness is not a very satisfactory principle of organization for the curriculum in English.

What is the school and college subject called "English"? This question the Commission took as its starting point. The report that follows provides an answer arrived at largely by discussion among its members and with hundreds of teachers. The answer rests on the unstartling assumption that language, primarily the English language, constitutes the core of the subject; and on the further and equally unstartling assumption that the study and use of the English language is the proper content of the English curriculum.

So simple and obvious an answer may seem too slight to justify elaboration into a formal report, but the perusal of scores of school curriculums has convinced the Commission that a simple answer is needed at the present time. The need can best be illustrated by a comparison. When the work of this Commission began, that of the College Board's Commission on Mathematics was coming to a close. What the mathematicians found in the school curriculum was a disciplined but largely anachronistic program of study, rigidified in its sequence and unresponsive to important developments in mathematical theory. They recommended drastic revisions in content, methods of instruction, and the ordering of elements. Their recommendations, in conjunction with those of other groups working on the same problem at the same time, and in conjunction with groups independently studying school curriculums in the sciences, have produced dramatic changes in less than 10 years. Where these recommendations have stimulated the development of new programs, it may reasonably be claimed that curriculums in mathematics and the sciences are "up to date."

For English the situation is quite different. "English must be kept up," wrote Keats; but keeping it up is not primarily a matter of keeping it up to date. To a large degree, the study of English or of any of those subjects loosely classified as "the humanities" is not a matter of making new, but of constant renewal, constant rediscovery, constant restoration. The sciences and mathematics lose their relevance if they fail to keep close to the working front of their disciplines. The humanities most often suffer from having their essence diluted or obscured by what appears to be new. This is not to say that current knowledge has no meaning for the humanities, but only to insist that the accumulation of the past is for them far richer than for the sciences. Yet, precisely because the humanities, the study of one's native language and literature among them, are so thoroughly implicated in everyday human activity, they are highly susceptible to immediate and ephemeral influences. The fashion of a time often so overlays them, particularly in their popular forms, that their real nature is all but lost sight of. The English curriculum in the average secondary school today is an unhappy combination of old matter unrenewed and new matter that rarely rises above the level of passing concerns. *Macbeth* vies with the writing of thank-you notes for time in the curriculum, and lessons on telephoning with instruction in the processes of argument.

The first job, then, of the Commission on English was to distinguish between the passing and the permanent, to affirm and describe the nature of English as a subject. In making its description, the Commission was well aware that a curriculum should in every case derive from a particular situation. It therefore quite deliberately chose to concentrate its attention on the program for secondary school students who are preparing for college. The Commission believes that the sooner the program in English for college preparatory students can be given sound underpinnings, the sooner corollary programs for other students can be thoughtfully designed. Even for college preparatory students, emphasis and curricular materials will and should vary from program to program, but the main concerns remain the same, and it is to them that the Commission has directed its attention. In choosing to describe only the English program for the college-bound student, it has simply adopted the principle of beginning work where resources are at present largest and where a solution may most readily be found.

The Problem of Preparing English Teachers

Approximately 100,000 men and women teach English in the 29,000 secondary schools of this nation. The requirements for certification to teach the subject vary widely from state to state. In those states where a "general high school certificate" is obtainable, no specific preparation is required. In those requiring subject certificates, the lowest standard calls for 12 hours of collegiate study in English, roughly two full-year courses or their equivalent; the highest calls for 36 hours, a little more than one-third of the usual college program. The average for all 50 states is between 16 and 18 hours—that is, between five and six semester courses. In most states, a teacher may be assigned to teach English, with or without formal preparation, for a minor portion of his teaching time; and in most a temporary certificate, renewable with or without evidence of subsequent professional study, may be issued with little or no regard for professional qualification in the subject if need for staff is great and qualified teachers are not available. The same condition prevails for teachers of other secondary school subjects, as well, but the tendency to staff English classes part or full time with teachers inadequately prepared for their work is especially prevalent. At the present time fewer than half of the English teachers in our schools can claim completion of a college major in their subject. That is the first aspect of the problem.

The second is no less serious. Because three or four years of English are required of all students in grades 9 through 12, the number of classes must be large; and the general practice is to economize by assigning to each class as many students as the classroom will hold. Average class size for English is 28, and most teachers are expected to teach five such classes a day. In addition, because they have an apparent connection with "English,"—in that they use language—dramatics, debate, public speaking, and school publications are normally part of the English teacher's extracurricular assignment.

In short, too much work is ordinarily required of teachers from whom, at the same time, too little professional preparation is expected.

The Professional English Teacher

Like any other professional person, the professional English teacher is one who has been trained, or has trained himself, to do competent work. For him professional competence should mean, at the minimum: a college major in English or a strong minor, preparation sufficient to qualify him to begin graduate study in English; systematic postcollegiate study, carried on privately or in a graduate school; a reading command of at least one foreign language, ancient or modern; a deep interest in literature, old and new, and a solid set of critical skills; the ability to write well and the habit of writing, whether for publication or not; a knowl-

5

edge of the development of the English language and familiarity with recent work in linguistics; a desire not simply to know but to impart knowledge; skill in the handling of instructional problems and knowledge of the research concerning them; an unflagging interest in the processes by which the young learn to use language effectively and richly.

Beyond these minimums, the professional English teacher may broaden his activity to include research, participation in the work of national and regional associations for the improvement of his field, study through summer institutes in his own and allied disciplines, help with community affairs (the improvement of the town library, adult education, and the like) for which his training makes him valuable. Yet, no matter how widely he engages in such activities, the core of his professional duty is in the classroom. If he does not fit himself to perform well there, whatever he does elsewhere will be less than enough. His work in the classroom demands the mind of an experienced professional and the heart of a devoted amateur, not those of someone tapped for the job because he has read some books and is known to have been speaking English all his life. He must serve at times as critic, historian, actor, preacher, literary and linguistic historian, and philosopher. Nothing less than thorough training and the commitment to continued study can prepare him for his work.

Given conditions proper for professional work, the teacher has responsibilities that can be quite clearly designated. He must, obviously, be properly trained for what he is to do. On this score, the training institutions—teachers colleges and the English departments of other colleges from which a great many secondary school English teachers come—are liable to serious criticism. It cannot be assumed, as it has been, that either random courses in literature and heavy emphasis on methodology, or a major consisting almost entirely of courses in literature, is adequate preparation for the teaching of secondary school English. A good part of that teaching will necessarily be concerned with composition, written and oral, and with the study of language; and only a small part of the work in literature will be devoted to a purely historical study, the kind most common in college English courses.

Even sound formal preparation does not guarantee, of course, that a teacher will be a good teacher, but it does give at least the assurance of a sound basis on which to build. It is, therefore, a serious matter that for more than half of those now teaching English in our secondary schools there is no such assurance. Some of that more-than-half may have done for themselves what their training institutions did not do; many are undoubtedly excellent teachers. Even so, in terms of professional standards for the 100,000 it takes to man English classrooms in our secondary schools, clear standards of preparation, if instituted and enforced, would guarantee a distinct improvement in the quantity and quality of knowledge purveyed in the classroom and, one can reasonably assume, in the mastery of the skills taught there.

Public Responsibility to the Teacher

It is unjust and uneconomical to impose conditions on a professional person that prevent him from doing professional work. An English teacher cannot teach the skills and art of composition if he has no time in which to read students' compositions carefully. He cannot teach students to read widely and well if books for such reading are unavailable and if capricious local censorship constantly restricts the range of books he may use or assign. He cannot explore with students the nature of their own language without the resource of unabridged and historical dictionaries and books on language. All this would seem obvious enough, yet it is commonplace for English teachers to be assigned five classes a day of 30 students or more; it is commonplace for them to have only two or three books to work with in class—an anthology, a grammar book, and perhaps a spelling workbook. It is rare to find an English classroom equipped, as it should be, with good dictionaries, a variety of books, recordings, and slides; it is equally rare to find a school library well enough equipped to serve more than a small portion of its students. These are not "frills" any more than scales and pumps and test tubes are frills in the laboratory. English is unlikely to be well taught without them, and the professional English teacher is seriously handicapped when they are not supplied.

It is clear that far too many English teachers have stopped serious reading, have stopped writing, have given up hope of getting anything more than pedestrian work done in their classes. If all were as strong as the strongest, they might manage to keep themselves professionally alert despite unreasonable class loads and exhausting after-class work with dramatics, debate, public speaking, and the school newspaper. Many, however, simply do not have energy enough to do all that must be done during the school day, much less the stamina to continue their labors fruitfully at night and over weekends. Until it is clearly understood by the public and by school administrators that harried teaching is ineffective teaching, the worth of a teacher's professional training will never be more than half realized in practice. If he is to do a competent job, the English teacher must not be expected to teach more than 100 students a day.

A simple calculation will show that such a schedule is anything but easy. If the teacher of 100 students assigns only one composition every two weeks, he will have 50 to read and comment on each week. Even the most expert cannot deal helpfully with a two-page theme in much less than 15 minutes; a reading that will be pedagogically useful to the student may take from 20 to 30 minutes. That activity alone, then, can mean from 12 to 20 hours of hard work. If conferences are to follow, as they should, especially on papers that require rewriting and reorganization, time for them must be added. And to that must be added time for preparation of lessons, for correcting tests, and for the necessary "household" activities that are part of every teacher's work. All this before assignments outside of classes, before committee work, before school projects. And all this before any allotment at all of time for private study and for critical thought about what one is doing. In an era of an ever shortening work week, the teacher's week has steadily grown longer and busier. This is the principal threat to professional teaching, especially to professional teaching in so time-consuming a field as English, and no community can afford to look on it as a matter of little concern. Hours in the classroom are exhausting, and working hours apart from it are, though in a different way, almost equally taxing. Teachers must not be hurried or harried if teaching is to be what it should be.

Recommendations to Improve the Quality of Instruction

For five years members of the Commission have talked and worked with English teachers in all parts of the country. Their inescapable conclusion from data and direct observation is that a high proportion—perhaps a majority—of English teachers know much less about their subject than they should know in order to teach it even reasonably well. The reasons for this condition are many and not easy to correct, but further decline is inevitable unless immediate efforts are made to improve training, to tighten certification requirements in subject study, and to make the English teacher's job more attractive.

The recommendations that follow represent not an ideal set of standards but a reasonable minimum for sound, vigorous teaching of secondary school English. Some school systems already require and provide more than these recommendations set forth, and the fact that their graduates regularly perform better than the average in national examinations such as the College Board Advanced Placement Examinations is evidence enough that these recommendations mark a level below which schools cannot operate without impairing the quality of instruction they offer.

Professional Standards

Certification standards in most states are far too low to guarantee that teachers admitted to the classroom are adequately prepared for the work they must do. The argument that short supply makes increased requirements impossible is self-defeating. Experience in other professions has shown that in the long run both quality and supply increase when requirements rise, because able students are attracted to those professions which set high standards for admission. Because the machinery of state certification is complex and difficult to change, the onus at present must fall on college and university English departments to set, independently, sound requirements for graduation with teaching certificates in English.

Recommendation 1. That certification to teach secondary school English be based on evidence of creditable work, at the minimum, of the following kinds:

> formal study of the history and structure of the English language
>
> study in rhetoric and composition above the level of the freshman course
>
> work in critical theory and practice with attention to bibliography and library resources
>
> at least one course in speech and the oral interpretation of literature
>
> two semester courses in American literature
>
> four semester courses in English literature, of which one should be the study of a single writer (preferably Shakespeare) in depth,

and of which others should represent approaches not exclusively historical

at least one course in English social and cultural history

enough study of one foreign language to guarantee reading facility.

Recommendation 2. That, in addition to the minimal requirements in subject matter, study in pedagogical processes include the following:

one course in the psychology of learning

one course in the methodology of the subject (selection of materials, lesson planning, curriculum development, review of relevant research)

one course in the history of American educational theory and institutions

one semester of full-time practice teaching under close and competent supervision.

Recommendation 3. That temporary certificates be valid for only one year at a time with renewal dependent on evidence of professional study, in the subject or in pedagogical processes, whichever may be lacking in the candidate's preparation to meet the requirements listed under Recommendations 1 and 2.

Recommendation 4. That school systems assume some responsibility for the expense of study beyond that required for certification, through stipends, tuition-free courses, and substantial salary increments.

Teaching Conditions

Although situations differ so greatly that what may be reasonable teaching conditions in one place will be unreasonably difficult in another, the consensus of English teachers is that unless a ceiling for the teaching assignment can be established (Recommendations 5 through 7) there is little hope for materially improved instruction.

Recommendation 5. That the English teacher be assigned no more than four classes a day.

Recommendation 6. That the average class size be no more than 25 pupils.

Recommendation 7. That the English teacher be responsible for supervision of no more than one continuing extracurricular activity during a school year.

Recommendations 8 through 11 go beyond teaching assignments to spell out provision for space, equipment, and clerical assistance that would be taken for granted in business or in another profession but are far too seldom available to the teacher.

Recommendation 8. That specific classrooms be set aside for the teaching of English.

Recommendation 9. That each of these classrooms be equipped with reference books and filing cabinets and wired for audiovisual machines, and that all English teachers have access to a record player, tape recorder, television set, slide machine, motion-picture projector, and an opaque or overhead projector.

Recommendation 10. That space be provided for an English office equipped with a typewriter and a duplicating machine, and that clerical assistance be available for the cutting of stencils and the production of teaching materials.

Recommendation 11. That in addition to the annual budget for the school library, at least $1 per student per year be allotted for purchase and rental of special materials in English (books, slides, photographs, special issues of magazines, films, and the like).

Curriculum

The catch-all character of many English programs results in confusion of purpose and diffusion of responsibilities, both inimical to good instruction. The recommendations that follow are reminders both to the teacher and the administrator that clarity of definition is of primary importance.

Recommendation 12. That the scope of the English program be defined as the study of language, literature, and composition, written and oral, and that matters not clearly related to such study be excluded from it.

Recommendation 13. That the English curriculum of a school or of a school system be the result of cooperative planning by the teachers engaged in teaching it, and that it represent a clearly defined sequence of study from grade to grade.

Recommendation 14. That significant data of students' performance (reading records, sample compositions, term tests) be accumulated in individual folders and passed on from year to year to successive English teachers.

The Commission's Instruments

Since 1959, in addition to taking active part in hundreds of local, state, regional, and national meetings, the Commission has made three instruments for direct communication with English teachers in the secondary schools. Each is briefly described below.

The Institutes

The most venturesome, the most expensive, and the most far-reaching of the Commission's instruments were the 1962 Summer Institutes in 20 host universities throughout the country. These institutes, attended by 868 secondary school teachers of English selected by the host universities on the basis of their ability, experience, and promise, were preceded by a Planning Institute in 1961 at which all who were to teach in the 1962 institutes made a common curriculum. In the summer of 1962 each institute participant took three graduate-level courses—language, literature, composition—at one of the host universities. In addition to the three courses, the institutes included workshops in which theory was translated into practice. Participants devoted several afternoons each week to workshop activity.

Inevitably the quality of the 20 institutes was uneven, and inevitably some miscalculations occurred, particularly in estimating the amount of work a six- or eight-week institute could accomplish. But the failings proved to be of comparative unimportance beside the successes, as the strong endorsements that have followed this initial series of institutes attest. The most convincing evidence of their success is the continuation, at local expense, of many of the original institutes through subsequent summers and the opening of others, on a similar plan, in universities not among the original 20. In the summer of 1965 the United States Office of Education under Title XI of NDEA will sponsor 105 Summer Institutes for Advanced Study for Teachers of English.

In the summer of 1963 the Commission sponsored and operated a Second Planning Institute for 40 of the most promising participants in the 1962 institutes, as recommended by the institute directors. The special task of these teachers was to examine critically the workshop program of the 1962 institutes and to find means of improving it. In effect, this institute has provided a corps of teachers equipped to teach courses or serve as workshop directors in future institutes which may be independently sponsored by colleges and universities or in the national program of institutes organized with federal support.

A list of participating universities and their personnel for the institutes appears in Appendix B.

Kinescopes

Early in its planning the Commission decided to sponsor a series of kinescopes (films usable either on 16mm moving-picture projectors or in television broadcasting stations). To demonstrate sound practices in the teaching of language, literature, and composition, the Commission has developed half-hour kinescopes in which experienced teachers of English offer specific guidance on various aspects of instruction. These films are available for the mailing cost only, for use in conferences, department meetings, study groups, and for individual viewing. The kinescopes have all proved so popular that as many as 60 copies of a single film may circulate at one time. Besides the kinescopes already in circulation, several are still unfinished, either unfilmed or in an editorial middle stage, and a few have only been commissioned. (See Appendix C.)

The Book of Examinations

End-of-Year Examinations in English for College-Bound Students, Grades 9-12, published by the College Board in the summer of 1963, consists of examination questions in language, literature, and composition, followed by students' answers ranging in quality from excellent to poor and by a detailed analysis and evaluation of each answer. The volume serves two purposes: it illustrates clearly for English teachers everywhere the general range of competence in essay answers written at each grade level, and it provides rich demonstrations of the response good teachers give to the compositions they read. By setting the same questions for his students, any teacher may judge by their answers how close to or far from a general standard of performance they are; or he may simply use the volume as a supplement to his own practice in theme reading. (See Appendix C.)

This Report

The present report brings to an end the official life of the Commission and the major part of its activity. The title, *Freedom and Discipline in English,* has a twofold derivation. It is borrowed from an essay by Alfred North Whitehead ("The Rhythmic Claims of Freedom and Discipline") to which reference is made in the section on composition. But it also declares the Commission's belief that the combination of these two elements, in a sense different from Whitehead's, is a key to better English teaching. Such a combination is implied throughout the report. For example, the Commission believes that schools and teachers should be free to choose what kind of grammar and what literary works are most appropriate for their own students, but that these choices will be effective only if the teachers have undergone the discipline of professional training, which many now lack.

In the sections that follow the Commission offers a statement about the teaching and learning of English to which it hopes the informed public and members of the profession can subscribe. Though it is too much to expect that there will be full agreement on all the issues, the Commission hopes that the point of view it has developed in five years of observation, discussion, and experimentation will prove acceptable, and that it can clarify thinking about the problems to which teachers of English in secondary schools and colleges must address themselves.

The report is written primarily to those who have immediate responsibility for the English program—English teachers above all, and their official colleagues: curriculum coordinators and school administrators. The Commission hopes, however, that what it says will be of more than passing interest to many others: to college English departments in which new teachers are trained, to state departments of education, and finally to those whose influence on the schools, for good or ill, is often decisive —active laymen.

Language

No elaborate justification is needed for the systematic study of language. Such study is a legitimate inquiry of great intrinsic interest. Pupils come to school with some competence in the speaking of English, and throughout their lives they continue to practice and perfect this skill. Learning the arts of reading and writing is a more formal matter, to a greater degree the result of study and instruction; but the teaching of these subjects must be built upon the pupil's competence in speaking and understanding his language. The first point to be made then (it is one that must be frequently repeated) is that this connection is intimate, and that total separation is neither desirable nor, ultimately, possible.

Like any other study, the study of language offers its own discipline— a discipline which, properly regarded, is as taxing and exact as that of geometry. Like other disciplines, too, it has its presiding assumptions and theories, some of which are discussed or alluded to in the pages that follow.

A Historical Note

Schools have long been committed to improving their pupils' command of language. They have specifically assumed responsibility for the teaching of reading and writing. Ordinarily they have also taken responsibility for the cultivation of socially acceptable spoken and written English, and even for determining standards of acceptability. Whatever the truth of the charge that they fail fully to meet their responsibilities, the schools are now for better or worse committed to these aims, and the public will not permit them to relinquish the obligation.

Language study is the most difficult part of the English curriculum to treat, primarily because attitudes toward it are largely determined by a totally prescriptive outlook on English usage and by subscription to a Latin-oriented grammar. On scholarly grounds such views are not adequate. Unfortunately many curriculum planners and administrators, the general public, and not a few teachers are only imperfectly aware of the extent to which the traditional approach to language has been challenged and modified in the past few decades.

A few historical notes will help to make the present situation more intelligible. In the past, language study concentrated heavily on grammar. The need for such study and the kind of grammar taught were largely determined in the Middle Ages and the Renaissance by preoccupation with the study of the classical languages rather than of the vernacular. As school populations grew and popular interest in Latin and Greek declined, grammatical study lost a part of its utility. But the grammar remained, scarcely modified in form, directed now to teaching students how to write acceptable compositions in English by following rules derived largely from "dead," and therefore static, languages. So conceived, the teaching of grammar was not always effective—it may indeed have been effective far less often than its proponents believed; yet it did offer an attempt to deal with the facts of language. Because it did that, and because it provided an intellectual discipline, it preserved for itself a respected place in the curriculum.

Hand in hand with prescriptive grammar went the concept of prescriptive correctness, of clear and identifiable distinctions between right and wrong in matters of idiom and usage. It did not greatly matter that even the most honored writers, present and past, sometimes ignored these prescriptions. What the arbiters and recorders of usage sought was a standard to which the skilled might assent and the unskilled aspire. There was a readily discernible need for such a prescriptive attitude in the nineteenth-century American school. Some educational discipline, however arbitrary, was needed both to refine the crudities of much frontier speech and to provide clear-cut models for the waves of immigrants whose native language was something other than English. Millions of people were desperately eager to discover an objective standard of correctness, and the prescriptive textbook and teacher provided it. And, since people looked to the grammarian as one who must be capable of describing each linguistic infelicity in a rigorous way, ideas about grammar and usage became inextricably confused. This confusion still prevails in many quarters.

Meanwhile, unperceived by all but a relatively small number of teachers in the secondary schools, the winds of revolutionary doctrine began to blow in the realm of language study. The traditional rules of grammar, the efficacy of parsing and diagraming, the clear alternatives between correct and incorrect usage were all boldly attacked and at least partially discredited.

The revolution began shortly after World War I with empirical demonstrations that traditional grammar, as conventionally taught, had relatively little effect on writing and was of negligible value in improving oral usage. The monographs of Sterling A. Leonard on the history of prescriptive attitudes toward English usage and on present-day usage raised similar doubts concerning standards of correctness. Leonard found a powerful ally in Charles C. Fries, who published in 1927 a stimulating and persuasive book, *The Teaching of the English Language,* designed as a text for the training of English teachers. The works of Fries and Leonard traced the evolution of the traditional rules, showing how those rules had developed in response to a specific set of intellectual and social conditions in eighteenth-century England. They also liberally documented the uncomfortable fact that the rules had never been an accurate reflection of usage, even that of the best writers. Both men took the point of view—accepted by the well informed in all ages—that usage is not stable but dynamic, and that, even at a given time, it is not uniform for all its educated users.

As early as the late 1800's, moreover, certain of the assumptions and methods of the traditional grammatical analysis of English had been challenged by such distinguished scholars as Henry Sweet and Otto Jespersen. The publication of Leonard Bloomfield's *Language* in 1933 stimulated a more intense study of English, modeled to a degree upon the methods and techniques of behavioristic psychology, and emphasizing initially, at least, the analysis of the spoken language. This came to be designated as the structuralist approach.

In the meantime, both the lexicographers and the dialect geographers had been refining their techniques for collecting valid samples of actual usage. The results of their work discredited even further the accuracy of many statements about the English language in the conventional school texts. Most recently the transformational grammarians have begun to challenge the analyses of their immediate predecessors. By the beginning of the present decade many of the older verities had vanished, and in their place appeared what must often have looked, to the layman, at least, like a new Babel.

All these developments have been noted in the professional journals, and all have been discussed in talks and in workshops at professional meetings. Moreover, the challenge to traditional methods has inevitably begun to affect the content of school textbooks. Some school systems have introduced new or greatly modified materials based on the procedures of structural linguistics. A few others are trying to use the quite dissimilar framework and techniques of transformational grammar. Innovation is the order of the day, and many of those educated in traditional methods and assumptions have grown uneasy or defensive about their practices. They have been told that their approach to language study, with a tradition of 150 years behind it, is no longer acceptable; yet they see little unanimity about a replacement. Though quite prepared to accept the obvious fact that literary critics disagree among themselves, as do poets, philosophers, and historians, they are reluctant to grant the same privilege to linguistic scholars. From them, teachers feel justified in demanding a unanimous set of answers to a series of pressing and practical questions: Is the teacher to abandon the traditional approach to grammar? What is he to replace it with, if he does? If new material of some kind is the answer, what is he supposed to do with it? Is it intended to be "useful," or is he to teach it simply because it is "interesting"? Unanimous or not, answers there must be, and the Commission has attempted to provide some in the pages that follow. First, however, something must be said about fundamentals of language learning and language study and about their implications for the school curriculum.

Language Learning in the Early Years

A modern view of language study must begin with the linguistic situation of the child as he starts his elementary school career. In mathematics, social studies, and science what he does in the first and second grades generally represents an introduction to a fresh subject; this is patently not true of his work in English. For three and possibly four years before he enters kindergarten, he has been expressing himself in speech and has been responding to what he hears. Three points need emphasis:

The child's school experiences with the spoken language extend his preschool experience rather than introduce him to a wholly new subject or skill.

Learning to read and to write is not a simple extension of preschool experience. It is learning a skill: how to control the writing system of English receptively and productively. For most children entering school, this is a wholly new endeavor. At least three or four years will be required to bring the child's reading proficiency to the level of his ability to speak and understand, and to make reading a means of enlarging his linguistic experience and competence. It will take still longer for him to write with reasonable competence.

Learning the language activities (listening, speaking, reading, writing) is not the same as learning about the structure of the language or its lexicon. The first is a development of a skill and depends upon exercise and habit. The second is reflective and highly conscious; it demands the ability to think abstractly and to perceive logical relationships.

In view of these observations, easily verified but often forgotten, it is necessary to consider afresh the nature of that responsibility for the student's competence in English which the schools have traditionally assumed. To be sure, two of the celebrated three R's have to do with language. Many teachers have been under the impression, however, that they can teach the language arts as directly and as objectively as they can teach geography or typing. But this view is inaccurate; it proceeds from a concept of language, or more commonly of grammar, as a subject matter consisting chiefly of rules and definitions that students should be able to master through memory and drill.

Acquiring one's native language is, in its beginning stages, largely informal and unconscious. Although no preschool child can rely on habitual responses to identify Thomas Jefferson or tell him that 63 is the product of 9 times 7, even at the age of 4 or 5 his language sense will tell him whether he should say, "Daddy came," or "Daddy is coming," "Bill hit the ball," or "The ball hit Bill." By the time he is ready for school, he can produce orally the basic patterns of the language, and he has a vocabulary that may run as high as 24,000 words.

Yet, by contrast, he is usually unable to read or to write even simple sentences. Very seldom can he do more than print his name in large ungainly letters. The teacher who begins teaching him to read and write must not overlook his skill in speaking and understanding, must instead be prepared to build upon that skill. More than that, the teacher must remember, as he seeks to accelerate the child's learning of language, that the process goes on outside the classroom as well as in it.

Almost from birth the child stretches to participate in the linguistic environment that surrounds him. He first enters it, perhaps, by curtailing the randomness of the sounds he produces, and bringing them closer to the speech sounds he hears. At about the same time he begins to understand in a rough way a few of the things his parents say. Eventually he attempts words, practices them, and perfects their use in context. As he develops, he extends his control to phrases and larger constructions, gradually adding them to his repertory of readily available responses—that is, making them habitual. As a result, by age 3 or so he can produce surprisingly long and complex sequences without great effort, and by age 5 he controls many, perhaps most, of the structural patterns of his language. Yet because a language is rich, he will continue to learn it throughout his lifetime; indeed he will probably never learn its entire structure, and certainly he will never learn its entire lexicon.

Along the way, a large part of what he learns is obligatory. After a numeral higher than 1, for instance, he will automatically use a plural noun form. He will automatically place an adjective indicating relative age before one indicating color—*old gray hat.* Without thinking about it, he will recognize that, in response to a statement, interrogatives such as *where, who,* and *what,* when spoken with a rising intonation, call for repetition ("I'm going down town." "Where?" "Down town."); when spoken with a falling intonation, for more specific information ("I'm going down town." "Where?" "To the shopping district."). Such obligatory patterns we all learn early in life and can produce or respond to without conscious attention.

But linguistic performance is by no means all obligatory. A good deal consists of choice—in diction, word form, sentence structure, the grouping or ordering of sentences in larger units. Such choices operate widely in speech, but they are especially important in writing, since substitutes must be found for such oral means of communicating as intonation, voice quality, or gesture, and since writing is judged by more elaborate standards. The written language is indeed something quite different from the simple transcription of speech. Its vocabulary, for example, differs in range and complexity; its syntax is more precisely ordered; coherence must be greater. Choice is at the heart of "style," and it is therefore of the first importance to the writer.

Learning to read effectively also demands sensitivity to choices, but of a different nature. The skillful reader learns to observe and judge the choices that the writer has made—though no reader ever succeeds in becoming attuned to all of them. It is possible, of course, to "over-read" a book, to imagine options that the writer never confronted.

Obviously, competence in speaking does not insure competence in reading and writing. What is the teacher to do? The natural procedure, it would seem, is to draw on the skill the student already has as an aid in developing the others he must acquire. Yet conventional practice suggests that until very recently no one has thought of grammar as being particularly relevant—certainly not as essential—to the teaching of reading in its early stages. Grammar seldom appears in the curriculum earlier than the fourth grade, when the initial and critical steps, from hearing and speaking words to recognizing them in print, have already been taken. Nor is it considered essential to the teaching of composition in its early stages. Thus by the time he reaches the fourth grade a student will normally have done a certain amount of both oral and written composition without knowing anything about formal grammatical analysis.

It is sometimes argued that the schools can safely ignore instruction in language, inasmuch as the student has both "learned" his grammar and taken his first steps in learning to read and write without the help of grammatical study. To that, the counterargument is that school instruction should reinforce, build upon, systematize what the student already knows so that he can make full use of it.

A distinction must be made between two senses of the word "grammar." In one sense, a child who learns to speak his language correctly can be said to know its grammar. In another sense—that of knowing the language of grammatical description—he may not know it at all even though he speaks the language well. Grammar in the second sense he may not encounter until the fifth or sixth year of school; grammar in the first sense is an essential aspect of his language learning.

For grammar as a matter of description, a second distinction is important—that between the study designed to give the student a concept of the structure and functioning of his language and that designed to clarify and fix a number of specific items of usage. What, in the end, is to be said for making formal study of language, especially of grammar, an important part of the English program?

The Debate about Teaching Grammar

At least four justifications for the teaching of grammar are frequently put forward:

1. Grammar study is necessary for, at least helpful in, the eradication of faults, and consequently it develops the power to read and write and speak well. The reference here is not to exercises in usage but to formal analysis, such as parsing verbs, labeling sentences, distinguishing syntactical components. This opinion, strongly held, has also been vigorously attacked. Many English teachers can cite instances in which improvement in writing and reading followed grammatical study. Because of their personal experience, even though that experience is less than definitive, the contrary conclusions of research may fail to convince them. It has been argued that the results of formal grammatical study in proportion to the time usually spent on it are disproportionately small: much input produces little output. But it may be as reasonably argued that if the grammar were more soundly based or more effectively presented, results would be better. It has also been said that if such instruction works at all, it works mainly for those of superior intelligence, but since this is just as true of instruction in literature, in mathematics, or in any other academic subject, it proves nothing.

Whatever the corrective value of studying linguistic structure, this activity must be sharply distinguished from direct classroom assaults on specific items of usage. Both the public and teachers often confuse the two; as a consequence they develop a mistaken and somewhat unrealistic view of grammar. To them it means power over the prestige dialect, and hence a way of achieving cultivation and of rising in the social scale. Thus the public tends to look upon any challenge to grammar as a debasement of culture and an evidence of social decay, which the school should combat as best it can. Yet the simple fact remains that any grammar is at least in part a description. As such, it is open to attack in two ways: critics may say that it describes the wrong thing (an inferior dialect), or that it does not square with the facts. Criticism of the second sort coming from linguistic scholars obviously should not be taken as an effort to undermine standards.

2. *Grammar study makes possible easier communication between teacher and student.* The teacher who is annotating a student's composition or discussing it with him, who is calling attention to something in a literary text, or who is discussing language as such is indeed helped if he can use the convenient terminological shorthand that grammars provide. Questions like "What happens if you move the participle?" or "How does that verb affect the attitude you have toward the statement?" are precise and efficient. If teaching is properly timed, if grammar is introduced when there is a real need to name language components, this benefit may certainly be gained in short order. Or, rather, such a result is dependable provided the student is not confused by a disparity between the definitions he learns and the facts as he observes them in the language

knows and uses. It is on this point that traditional grammar as generally found in school textbooks is most often challenged.

3. Grammar study is necessary as preparation for the study of foreign languages. This justification is frequently advanced, and there is undoubtedly some virtue in it. Surely it is not unreasonable to maintain that familiarity with one mode of analysis makes the learning of similar modes of analysis somewhat easier. Of course it is true that the grammars of no two languages, even of those within the Indo-European family, are identical. Thus, for example, inflections in English are few and word order is vital for meaning, while in Latin inflections are many and word order is largely rhetorical. Nevertheless a knowledge of English grammar provides a base from which to move, and it becomes more important as the position of foreign-language study in the schools constantly grows stronger.

4. Grammar study is a good discipline. Since any systematic study is good discipline, the question is whether, as a discipline, grammar has something to recommend it over other systematic studies. Is it as likely as any other, or more likely than most, to contribute to mental alertness and precision, to sensitivity, to appreciation of order? It is fair to say that potentially it has those capabilities. As it is often taught, it does not realize them. Where grammatical study is largely rote learning and nothing more, where diagraming and parsing and workbook underlining are an end in themselves, the discipline they provide is neither invigorating nor liberalizing. Grammar well taught is not training in the exercise of memory but training in perception and in relation, for a teacher cannot expect students to use grammar toward the improvement of their reading and their writing unless he constantly relates it to these activities. To do so is far more than to require that next week's composition contain three complex sentences and one example each of adjectival and adverbial phrases. Only when options are apparent, when the connection between the choice made and the meaning and character of the whole is given proper attention, will grammatical study earn its keep as a discipline.

To these justifications, at least two more should be added. One is akin to the first given above but places the emphasis otherwise. Although every normal child, even when left to his own devices, learns control of an amazingly rich and complex linguistic system, his dialect inevitably differs from the one recorded in most books, magazines, reports, and so on, which may be called "edited English." The study of grammar can help him to master this unquestionably valuable dialect, for use alongside his own as the occasion demands. Given certain aspirations, he may even want to relinquish his own dialect in favor of "edited English."

Grammatical analysis makes it possible to familiarize the student with structures not included in his own dialect. It is easy, for instance, to extend the competence he probably displays in using sentences like "I was glad the speech was so short" and "The speech disappointed me," so that he can also use constructions like "That the speech was brief disappointed no one." Again, grammatical analysis is a short way to systematic understanding of the discrepancies between casual syntax and formal syntax. No appeal to snobbery is required to suggest the importance, both for individual students and for society, of learning and preserving a public idiom.

The other additional justification has something in common with the third and fourth stated above but deserves independent mention: an intelligent study of grammar reveals surprising and interesting things about the orderliness of what the child has learned in a nonorderly way —his own language. It can reveal at least some facts about the structure of language in general. And it can tell a good deal about the way the human mind works. Ideally, then, though too rarely in practice, the study of grammar has great intrinsic value and intellectual appeal, aside from practical benefits.

This survey of the arguments leads to no very novel conclusion: since grammatical study can be both illuminating and useful, it should ordinarily be made a part of the curriculum in such a way as to exploit its potential usefulness. This means that learning the names of grammatical elements should coincide with the use of those names in meaningful activity, not in drill for the sake of drill; that complexities of syntax should be identified and their functions made apparent as they are encountered, as well as in anticipation of such encounters; that constant application rather than yearly review should be the means of keeping grammatical knowledge and terminology active; that in the upper years of the secondary school, the knowledge of grammar should be persistently employed to increase the student's awareness of options in his own writing and his sensitivity to the options taken in the literature he reads.

The case for grammar is strong; nevertheless a warning is in order here. If those who have the interests of the entire English program at heart insists upon emphasizing utility as the sole criterion for including language study in the curriculum, they may find themselves in a position where they will have to defend the study of literature on the same grounds. There is a lesson to be learned from the unhappy experience of those who urged the substitution of modern languages for Greek and Latin with arguments based on practicality and usefulness, only to find French, German, and Spanish judged by the same criterion and found wanting in the decades of the thirties and forties. Humanists are ill advised to put all their eggs in the basket of utility.

It must be granted that a good command of standard spoken and written English can be acquired without the aid of grammatical analysis or formal instruction in usage, semantics, and the use of the dictionary. An acquaintance with children reared in homes where the prestige dialect is spoken reveals clearly that such children have developed automatic responses to so wide a variety of language situations that they are guilty of few lapses, even under the strain of satisfying difficult or unfamiliar demands on their resources. But this evidence provided by the ideal situation has little relevance to the problems of the classroom in many American communities.

It has already been remarked that social conditions have greatly affected the teaching of English in the past. Modern schools still face a very complex problem. A considerable proportion of the children in elementary grades come from homes in which standard English does not prevail. Some, indeed, come from homes in which English is not even the family language; their speech is bound to be a combination of what they are taught at school and what they pick up in association with others. In addition, they are exposed to the argot of the streets and the infelicities of much mass communication. As if such diverse factors were not enough for the teacher to cope with, there is another—the variety permissible within the standard language.

Yet there can be no serious question about the responsibility of the English teacher—though certainly it is not solely his—to bring his students to the point where they can easily use the standard language. The difficulty is not in defining his responsibility but in determining on what grounds and by what means he is to exercise it.

Problems of Usage

Reference has already been made to the central problem, that of the instability of language itself. For reasons little understood or too complex to identify distinctly, language changes perceptibly even from decade to decade, lingering in one form here, altering swiftly elsewhere. Grammar books often lag and sometimes contradict respectable contemporary usage. The use of *like* as a conjunction is a case in point. Any good historical dictionary will validate that use in impeccable sources dating back for hundreds of years. And it can still be heard (as well as found in printed texts) on every hand, again from sources above reproach. Yet school textbooks almost unanimously disapprove it, and meticulous speakers generally avoid it. Examples of this kind are not uncommon. To cite one more instance, the requirement that after a negative the co-ordinate conjunctions be "so...as" rather than "as...as" is well fixed in standard texts and largely ignored outside them. How can this discrepancy between what the textbooks recommend and what the English-speaking world tolerates be dealt with?

First of all, the English teacher must know the facts about usage, what it really is at present in all its variety and what it has been. He must expect, and not resent, some change in "acceptable forms" and be prepared to see certain of his own cherished discriminations ignored by most literate folk. On the basis of the most trustworthy data that he can find—and it is important that he learn to employ the scholarly sources of such data intelligently—he must decide whether or not the item in question is in current use by those who are carrying on the affairs of the English-speaking world. Thus he may properly insist that dual or multiple negatives ("He couldn't hardly do it") be avoided, and that "he laid down on the bed" is entirely unacceptable, while he tolerates "presently" as an equivalent for "now." His responsibility drives him into what someone has aptly called "the briar patch of English usage," and he must expect to get scratched from time to time. Even so, he certainly cannot ignore the challenge, and he need not despair. His salvation lies in making students aware, as he himself should be aware, of the real nature of usage: that it characterizes social and economic levels, variety of occasion, and cultural attitudes even more than it reflects efficiency or subtlety of communication. He may often make a useful start by examining with his pupils the dialects exemplified in their own habits of speech. The fact that pronunciations and vocabularies vary, or that the canons of usage are unstable, should not deter him, nor should the fact that any particular locution may be obsolete in a hundred years.

The teacher must be careful to avoid the confusion that often arises between levels of usage and functional varieties of the language. Whether a particular locution is standard or substandard may be a matter of usage level; the distinction between speech and writing is one of functional variety. *Colloquial,* properly interpreted, is a label indicating a functional variety, not a level of the language, nor was the term, as used by lexicographers, ever intended as a condemnation. In addition he must take into account the effect upon language of various styles of discourse, recently characterized by one scholar as ranging from intimate to casual, consultative, and formal English. Each of these has its characteristic features, and what is appropriate to one style may be egregious in another. Not all these complexities need be taught, but they are matters concerning which the teacher and the taught cannot afford the luxury of ignorance. The teacher should remember, too, that grammatical analysis exerts no appreciable control over usage; usage frequently changes despite "grammar," and when it does, so must the grammar that describes it.

Certainly arguments over matters of usage, in the professional journals and elsewhere, have been more often characterized by heat than by light. Yet the number of disputed usages—those on which the textbooks disagree with each other or with current practice—does not seem to total more than two- or three-score items. It should not be difficult for any teacher to determine in what combinations of functional variety and style each of them fits, and where it is patently inappropriate. Nor should he overlook the fact that the formal item in the informal situation is just as much out of place as the informal in the formal. What the student should come to realize is that effective writers and speakers select their language purposefully, to fit the situation at hand, and what the teacher must realize is that no handbook is a substitute for linguistic sensitivity.

If a substandard usage is to be corrected, the standard usage must be made to replace the automatic response the child developed when he was learning his language. A grammatical explanation may occasionally help, and so may drill; but the change will not easily occur unless the child is properly motivated. Treating the matter as a moral issue is as impractical as it is improper, and making the issue that of social status or the prospect of satisfying a putative employer is often unrealistic and no more likely to be effective. The teacher's only reasonable position is one of explicitness: in school work the particular usage expected and required should be intelligently determined and clearly stated, and nothing else permitted to pass muster.

In a full view of the teaching of language, the continuing arguments about grammar and usage tend to obscure as much as to clarify the central issue. The heart of the matter for the English teacher is that he cannot approach the teaching of the native language in the way the mathematics teacher can approach the teaching of algebra. At best, he only assists the student in learning, and often in unlearning some of what he has learned. In order to do so, he shows the student how to be conscious of the choices he has learned to make. One of the more familiar devices for developing such awareness of language is called "grammar." If a language allows a great variety of choices, a grammar of English may be thought of in part as an inventory of the choices open to a user of the language.

The number of choices, or options, available to an educated speaker or writer of English is in fact infinite. As has already been pointed out no existing grammar describes them all or was ever meant to do so, though such completeness is a proper goal for linguistics. So-called "traditional" grammar was originally intended to establish a relationship between the analysis of English and that of the classical languages, so that the latter could be more easily taught. The techniques of structural grammar developed in part as a means of analyzing unwritten languages and of providing alphabets for them, functions it has often performed admirably. Transformational grammar does not lay any claim to immediate application, but its adherents consider it a more adequate theory of linguistic structure than previous grammars provide.

In perspective, all existing grammatical approaches to the English language fall somewhat short of dealing satisfactorily with problems of language that arise in secondary schools. At best each provides some tools for coping with the problems but not a full technique for solving them. Some of the present confusion among teachers stems from a misunderstanding about what these or any other grammars can do. In effect, schools have been giving their students tools in the expectation that the students themselves will work out the necessary techniques for using them. As so often happens, the gifted and the experienced can work with the crudest instruments, whereas the novice and the slow learner remain helpless with the best. What the student needs is far too often what he is not given.

Consider, for example, the fact that in most grammar books now in use morphology and syntax are the points of major emphasis. Since a good many students beginning grammar already possess an effective control of the principal inflectional and word-order patterns of English, such a book offers the student little more than a limited externalization of what he already knows, the obligatory parts of his language. Yet if it is to do anything, the study of language ought to show him how a sentence operates, both in speech and in writing—why and how, for instance, skillful writers avoid dangling modification, ambiguous reference, arbitrary tense and subject shifts, and so on. It ought to reveal to him ways of expanding and varying the patterns he already has. He needs to put to use what he knows, not just in order to know he knows it, but in order to create and understand complex structures of language, particularly as they appear in thoughtful writing. No rudimentary recapitulation of what he knows by habit, however often it may be repeated, will do that for him.

Preparation for Teaching Language

Before the proper aims of language teaching can be realized, two needs must be met. Neither is at all impossible of fulfillment. First, English teachers must be equipped with adequate knowledge about and an adequate understanding of the nature and history of the English language. Second, textbooks and other materials appropriate to the ends sought must be developed and made more generally available.

A satisfactory program of instruction for prospective teachers of English in the secondary schools is not difficult to outline. The first need is for study of the elements of language: phonology, morphology, syntax, and the lexicon. Although all four are important, the traditional emphasis on syntax and morphology should be lightened in order that more attention may be given to phonology and the lexicon, concerning which there is a good deal of ignorance. Even a rudimentary acquaintance with English phonetics can give a teacher a wholly new, productive (and perhaps even compassionate) understanding of the vagaries of English spelling, while some knowledge of stress and intonation can be of considerable value to his teaching of poetry.

The schools must constantly face the problem of vocabulary, and especially that of its enlargement through the introduction of new words as a result of technological developments and changes in social relationships. How does one make up new words out of old linguistic materials? How are words from other languages adapted to fit the forms and patterns of English? At successive stages in the history of the English language, various people have objected to words like *presidential, reliable,* and *television*. What principles govern "right" and "wrong" here? Perhaps no language has ever been called on to respond to so many situations as English has, and without some understanding of lexical principles even the native user may sometimes despair of striking a decent balance between rigidity and chaos.

A second requirement for the teacher is that of familiarity with the purposes, principles, and procedures of the various approaches to English grammar. Even the threefold division used here—traditional, structural, and transformational—constitutes something of an oversimplification. The so-called traditionalism of the old-style review grammar or workbook bears no resemblance to the fine work of Henry Sweet or Otto Jespersen, who are somewhat loosely and incorrectly classified as traditionalists, nor is the structuralism of Henry Lee Smith and George L. Trager at all like that of Charles C. Fries. Transformational grammar, still in its infancy, is changing rapidly. It should be admitted, then, that linguistic science at the moment can hardly provide the English teacher with a unanimously accepted grammar. The situation is of course disturbing, no more so to English teachers than to linguists themselves. The latter are working toward a unified theory of grammar, and there are signs that success will reward their efforts before long. If so, much of the grammatical theory and description that a teacher of English can learn now will have to be rectified or rejected in 10 or 20 years. But these remarks should not be taken as a counsel of despair. In some ways the English teacher's position resembles that of the physics teacher 40 years ago, who could ill afford to ignore both Newtonian mechanics and relativity theory just because they were in some ways at odds. Teachers of English should know enough about current problems in grammatical theory so that they can understand the resolutions that evolve, and they should know enough about the several descriptions of English so that they can draw freely upon each at points of relevance in the classroom.

Still another essential for the teacher is a sound, if not comprehensive, knowledge of the history of English. Here a broad acquaintance with the nature and causes of language change, both in the past and present, is of greater importance than a legion of minute details. Certainly the teacher should be able to understand the English of Chaucer and his contemporaries, of Shakespeare and his, and to describe the most striking differences between the language of Milton or of Fielding and that of Hemingway.

He should also understand the nature of usage, the forces affecting it, the areas of greatest instability, the characteristic directions of development. How interpretations of the doctrine of usage have undergone marked changes over the past 50 years has already been described, and our insights are continuing to change. A neat list of "good" and "bad" expressions, like those offered in many secretarial schools, is of little use; what is wanted is an understanding of currently accepted principles.

Some consideration must also be given to the problem of meaning. Some years ago a number of colleges began to offer courses in "general semantics" which dealt in a one-sided manner with the questions of emotive meaning and reference. Admittedly, a clear comprehension of the function of connotation and denotation is vital in literature and composition, but the prospective teacher must never suppose that language begins and ends there.

A final requisite, perhaps fully as important as any of the others, is an understanding of the nature and function of an up-to-date dictionary, a resource more valuable than any textbook—or several textbooks. It is a resource book in phonology and lexicon, and important also in morphology. Its usefulness for the study of usage, semantics, and the historical development of individual words is potentially great; and the more important dictionaries of the English language have explained in their introductory pages how they present such matters. The teacher must not be content simply to know that such resources exist; he must also be able to exploit them with complete proficiency in the classroom.

How much time would such instruction for the teacher require? A two-semester course offering a total of six credit hours, if efficiently organized and intelligently presented, should cover most of the basic matters. In view of all an English teacher must be able to do when he faces his class, it appears that not much more than this amount of time can be given to his preparation for training in language. English departments (from which a considerable number of majors graduate and become secondary school English teachers) have a clear responsibility in the matter and must recognize it. Their complaints about the ignorance of freshmen reflect no credit on their own program if the teachers of those freshmen were taught in their own departments.

The development of better textbooks and other materials is, at least from the point of view of most publishers, a matter of demand. When they are asked for by enough teachers, they will quickly become available. In the meantime, fortunately, many teachers are undertaking to make materials for their own use, and some publishers are sponsoring experimental texts designed to meet such needs as they discern. Certainly there is a great need at present for a really good secondary school rhetoric, a book or series of books in which all the resources of language study would be directed toward the literary uses of language in reading and writing. On the whole the textbook situation looks more promising than it has for some time, and there seems to be every indication that it will improve.

In conclusion, it is reasonable to maintain that the study of language has a justifiable place in the school curriculum, that it can be illuminating, and that it should be pursued in such a way as to take advantage of its potential usefulness. The responsibility for accomplishing these results rests ultimately with the indivdual school system and can be stated very explicitly. Improvement in the program depends largely upon improvement in the preparation of the teaching staff. Whether this is achieved through in-service or preservice training is immaterial; in all probability both means will have to be employed.

It follows that if those directing a school system believe it desirable to move from the familiar traditional methods in the direction of one or another of the newer developments, they should provide on their staff one or more English teachers fully competent to handle the appropriate grammatical and other linguistic techniques, and willing not only to teach them to students but to interpret them to other members of the department. If a school system does not have such teachers, it must acquire them or provide intensive training for those it has. Any curricular change that runs as deep as this must be made gradually, deliberately, and with a sincere commitment; it should not be a mere gesture toward modernity.

The school that is without immediate resources in staff for making a change, or is hesitating over the advisability of making one, ought perhaps to wait a few years while other schools, more richly endowed, or perhaps only more adventurous, work out problems of adaptation and sequence. Out of this experimentation will come, and already are coming, materials that show the mark of the classroom as well as of the study. By the end of this decade it should be possible for any school system convinced of the desirability of change to make preparations for it, confident that it will not find itself two or three years later wandering in mists of confusion.

In the meantime, a great deal can be done to make the study of language more effective than it has commonly been, quite irrespective of the grammatical system being used. And again success here will depend upon thoroughly prepared and dedicated teachers who can be made to feel that they have the support of the school administration, the policy-making body, and the community at large. No day in an English class need go by without enlarging the students' understanding of their language; no day should go by without the teacher's requiring students to put their understanding of language to effective use. Language is the richest acquisition of the human race, and the school should do all it can to make language the resource it can be.

Literature

A Curriculum Arrived at by Consensus

The secondary school English teacher is presumed to know various literary works and to be able to teach them well. What are they? If the Commission could claim for the study of literature a definiteness as apparent as that of other subjects in the curriculum, it might specify them; but all attempts to prepare a canon of literary works deserving a special place in the secondary school curriculum meet serious obstacles. Who can claim the authority to draw up any such master list? Or to require it, once drawn? Even granting satisfactory answers to those questions, one must face others no less troublesome. What conceivable principles can govern inclusion and exclusion? What effects would ensue from precise curricular prescription?

Proponents of a national curriculum have some persuasive arguments. Such a curriculum, prepared by highly competent people, would protect the study of literature from the ephemeral, the merely fashionable, and the patently trivial. It would make possible a sequence in which each year's study would lead clearly to the next. It would give all students in the United States a common literary culture, necessarily limited in range and inevitably variable in quality, yet substantial enough to provide a ground of reference for all. And, incidentally, it would sharply simplify the problem for national testing agencies and for college admissions boards.

None of these arguments is inconsiderable, and indeed they have prevailed in many countries in the world. They have prevailed, however, in particular situations and at costs that the proponents seldom mention. A national curriculum, in English or in any other subject, implies highly centralized control of education. In the United States, responsibility for education is constitutionally vested in the separate states, and it has been historically delegated largely to subdivisions of the state, to counties or

42

even to individual villages. Whatever advisory and research help may come from the federal government, the responsibility and the control lie elsewhere and will continue to do so. That alone makes talk of a national curriculum rather empty. And other counterarguments readily appear. To begin with, wherever they are in force national curriculums tend to stifle experimentation, limit inventiveness, and hinder, if they do not actually prevent, adaptation to local needs. They narrow rather than broaden the range of exploration and thereby may discourage imaginative people from entering the teaching profession. They retard the introduction of what is new, a matter less vital perhaps to English than to the sciences but still important even to English, for the atmosphere of constraint is infectious. Besides these known effects, another—less certain but entirely possible—must be faced: the total effect of mass media in the past 30 years has been to homogenize our culture; a national curriculum might well confirm rather than counter this on the whole undesirable process—confirm it on a higher level, without doubt, but confirm it all the same.

The arguments for curricular independence are implied in those presented against a national curriculum: opportunity for experiment, for inventiveness, for adaptation to local need; responsiveness to new knowledge; continuation of the pattern of direct public responsibility. To cite the arguments is to suggest the dangers, and it is against such dangers as inchoateness, lack of rigor, narrow and purely prudential interests, and misguided freedom that critics rightly aim their charge. At the same time anyone who argues for independence must face the fact that its advantages are more often sung than sought. By and large, English teaching today is less noticeably affected by remote curriculum makers than by textbooks chosen or assigned for classroom use. The evidence of syllabuses makes clear that too many teachers are letting textbooks do their curricular thinking for them. The problem, then, is partly that of finding a way to ensure the advantages of curricular independence without succumbing to the dangers implicit in it; and partly that of encouraging teachers to make good use of the very real freedom they have.

The Search for a Consensus

The Commission's proposed answer to the question "What literature should the English teacher know and teach?" is not a definition, not a master list, and not a description of the bewildering variety of activities of English departments. What the Commission seeks is a clearer understanding of the consensus that it believes already exists, though it is nowhere fully realized. Such a consensus on the teaching of literature should describe what professionally qualified teachers at different levels of instruction, in different schools and regions, can agree to take for granted about the teaching of literature.

Broadly speaking a consensus means an agreement arrived at through consultation and common consent. In their search for a *consensus gentium,* seventeenth- and eighteenth-century philosophers tried to state a few basic propositions about the nature of truth and the nature of nature —propositions that men everywhere agreed were true because they knew them by "common sense," by virtue of their common humanity, their common rationality. The same idea is implicit in the Declaration of Independence. There the truths that support an open and pluralistic society are called "self-evident" and are general, simple, and of infinitely varied application. Because English as a subject is necessarily wide and pluralistic, it, too, can be better understood through consensus than through definition.

Where a Consensus is Found

Where is this consensus to be found? It is not laid up in a heaven of expert generalizations. It can only be where the teaching of English is

44

going on, and it will be most authoritative in departments of English where teachers with a strong sense of their professional identity are joined in a common pursuit. It will be neither authoritative nor effective in departments staffed by teachers inadequately trained, lacking the judgment that should come from experience, or afraid of their responsibilities.

By a department we mean a group of teachers who share common but not identical professional backgrounds, common but not identical interests, abilities, and aims. In such departments, through collaboration and conversation, teachers can and do invent a rich variety of ways to reach their common aims and to teach a generally agreed-upon curriculum. Their diversity is their strength, their safeguard against any attempt to define one "right" list of books and to prescribe one "right" way of presenting them. Diversity becomes fragmentation only in a department where teachers are unsure of their professional preparation or find communication with their fellow teachers about curriculum futile in the face of prescribed lesson plans and graded textbooks. Where there is no meeting ground for study and discussion, and where teachers are poorly trained for their work, the imposition of a purely formal consistency may appear to be a bulwark against anarchy. But bad conditions are not reduced by such shoring up. Only the deliberate assignment of responsibility to those who must in fact exercise it can correct insularity and slavish adherence to a textbook. Within a flexible framework of order and responsibility the dangers arising from diversity are surely far less than those arising from curricular rigidity and professional suffocation.

The Role of Textbooks

Lacking a clearly understood consensus, teachers may rely on a textbook or series of textbooks that relieve them of the work of creating their own courses. When soundly conceived and responsibly edited such text-books have understandable appeal for the overburdened English teacher. At their best they present good texts attractively, arranging them usually by literary types, by themes, by a literary-historical plan, or by some combination of plans. They outfit the insecure teacher with auxiliary information and suggestions. They attempt to follow principles of gradation and integration of subject matter. In schools where the English department has arrived at no consensus, where teachers remain isolated from one another, and where regular professional cooperation within English departments and with teachers in other subjects is rare, reliance upon responsibly produced textbooks may be a necessity. But it is not a happy one. This is not to say that textbooks are of service only to in-secure teachers in ossified departments. A vigorous, freely cooperating department will use textbooks to carry out the agreed-upon purposes of a specific course. It will not, however, permit textbooks to dictate curriculum; it will not limit study to what can be found in any given text or series of texts. In the past 15 years, the emergence of a great paper-back-publishing industry has opened the way for diversification in even those schools where money is hard to come by. Today no department need confine itself to a single text on the ground of economy.

The Flexible Curriculum as a Reflection of a Continually Evolving Consensus

Every English teacher knows that owning a book is not necessarily the same thing as making that book his own. And every English teacher gradually develops a private library of books he has made his own by careful study. The literature in this private library (whether the teacher actually possesses the books or not) is usually made up of major and minor classics written in English, and the histories, biographies, and works of criticism that have helped the teacher to make this literature

46

his own. Although no two private libraries are identical, among them there is enough in common to make possible the beginning of a consensus.

Since the English curriculum can only be what teachers know, it starts with these private libraries. Fully formulated, it represents a pooling of all the teachers' resources, an emblem of the common work of an English department created by an association of teachers out of the works they care enough for to have made them their own. Just as the books a teacher has made his own will differ according to the educational background and individual taste of the teacher himself, so the English curriculum will differ from school to school. To accept the fact of unavoidable variety is merely to recognize that curriculums in literature must respond to the needs and interests of teachers and students in varying communities and in changing times. In the individual curriculum of a particular school—or of a school system—the achievable consensus on literature finds its center. The professional competence to build the curriculum, the institutional authority to teach it, and the responsibility for teaching it well exist only within English departments —and at no other educational or administrative level. The excellence of the curriculum is the measure of how fully the teachers within departments exercise their professional powers.

The Content of the Curriculum in Literature

What specifically does such a consensus imply about the content of the curriculum in literature? One implication is that it consists mainly of American and English literature, because this literature is what all English teachers are likely to know systematically and at first hand. Along with major and minor classics it will certainly include a selection of more recent books. These may or may not become part of the classic heritage, but they are important because literature does not possess abso-

47

lutely fixed values and because the classic heritage must be understood as an evolving tradition, open at one end.

Specific questions on the content of the curriculum can be resolved by asking: What would the professionally competent English teachers in a given department include or exclude? For example, would they include Chaucer, Shakespeare, Milton, Fielding, Pope, Keats, Dickens, Emerson, Thoreau, Browning, Dickinson, Arnold, Shaw, Twain, Conrad, James, T. S. Eliot, Auden, Faulkner, Hemingway? Most would agree to all these and many more. But which of their works? Almost certainly not *Troilus and Cressida,* nor *Cymbeline,* nor *The Essay on Man,* nor *Sordello.* But quite certainly *Gulliver's Travels,* the odes of Keats, *Huckleberry Finn,* and some of the short stories of Conrad and Hemingway. The criteria that make such works part of the teacher's library are the same as those that make them part of the curriculum: variety in kind, richness in content, expertness in execution. To those criteria, one must be added to take account of the difference in age and experience between teacher and student—the criterion of suitability, which makes *Sordello* a dubious choice and *The Return of the Native* an obvious one.

Does a consensus on the central importance of American and English literature exclude foreign literature in translation? Not entirely. Some works written in languages other than English come through the precarious route of translation with such force as to command and deserve attention. Preeminently, the Bible has become a part of "English," a part of our common culture, a part of our common humanity. In the King James Version it is a work of high literary merit and the source of more literary allusion than any other book in the language. To ignore the Psalms, the Song of Solomon, the great trial of Job, the subtle epistles of Paul is to ignore some of the best literature we have. On the same score, the greatest writers of any country, if well translated into English, merit inclusion if time, audience, and usefulness justify it.

Such catholicity does not automatically imply a course in "world literature." Since poetry and eloquence—sometimes even literal meanings—rise only with difficulty over the barriers of differing languages, and since few teachers are qualified to teach world literature with competence and authority, such courses do not belong securely to the English curriculum. This does not mean that literature should not be read and studied in translation or that a course in "Great Books" may not be justifiable for advanced and able secondary school students. But surely the study of world literature is not an acceptable alternative to a study of English and American literature.

Fairy tale, myth, and legend, however, belong in a special category. They constitute a literature not wholly or even mainly native to English, and they belong to no single literary tradition. They support and enrich our understanding of recurrent patterns of thought and action, as well as our capacity to grasp and understand an allusion. Familiarity with this "literature behind the literature" begins even in the stories and games of early childhood. Legend and myth seldom become a subject of sustained, formal study in the secondary school, but the reading of them should precede and accompany the study of more formal literature.

Claims are frequently advanced for the use of so-called "junior books," a "literature of adolescence," on the ground that they ease the young reader into a frame of mind in which he will be ready to tackle something stronger, harder, more adult. The Commission has serious doubts that it does anything of the sort. For classes in remedial reading a resort to such books may be necessary, but to make them a considerable part of the curriculum for most students is to subvert the purposes for which literature is included in the first place. In the high school years, the aim should be not to find the students' level so much as to raise it, and such books rarely elevate. For college-bound students, particularly, no such concessions as they imply are justified. Maturity of thought, vocabulary, syntax, and construction is the criterion of excellence in literature, and that criterion must not be abandoned for apparent expediency. The competent teacher can bridge the distances between good books and the immaturity of his students; that is, in fact, his primary duty as a teacher of literature.

The Organization of the Curriculum in Literature: Problems of Timing, Sequence, and Articulation

A skillful architect considers not only the form and materials for the structure he is designing. He must also reckon with the needs, the tastes, the level of sophistication of those who will occupy the finished building. The same is true in the designing of a curriculum in literature for students who have reached different degrees of maturity and who are reading at different stages of sophistication. In other words, once the teachers have decided which works are to have a place in the four-year curriculum for their school or school system, they must confront two questions: To which students should they teach them, and when?

Even though specific decisions about timing and sequence will differ, a fair consensus is discernible. Carlyle once observed that in literature the child or primitive man requires only to see an action going on, the more refined person wishes to be made to feel, and the most sophisticated man wants to be made to think. For an English department concerned with developing a sound sequential program in literature, these distinctions may be suggestive, though the stages do not, in fact, succeed one another in such a neat pattern that a curriculum can be based on them alone.

What is needed in addition is the common sense of experienced teachers who know their students well. At what grade level, for instance, should students read *The Odyssey*—sixth, ninth, eleventh, freshman year in college? Should Hemingway's *The Old Man and the Sea* be taught to ninth graders or to twelfth graders in advanced placement courses? Does *Ethan Frome* belong in the eighth grade or the eleventh? Are tenth grade, eleventh grade, and twelfth grade the sanctified places for *Julius Caesar, Macbeth,* and *Hamlet,* respectively, as custom and the anthologies seem to say? While it is undeniable that some works will yield much through reteaching at different grade levels, economy of time suggests that as much or more will be gained by single careful placement in the curriculum. Such placement will be determined partly by considerations of length and familiarity of setting and situation, even more by the degree of linguistic difficulty and the subtlety of insight required for rich understanding. The sequence for a particular school or school system will, then, reflect careful appraisal of the students to be taught, not to match their current competence and maturity but to move steadily though gradually ahead of it.

Kinds of Literature Courses

The usual ways of setting up a course in literature are by a chronological-historical survey; by themes; and by literary types. Each has advantages; none is free from pitfalls; and all will work in the hands of skillful teachers in a responsibly staffed English department.

The Historical Pattern: This method has the advantage of simplicity and clarity. If properly used, it enables the student to see something of the development of literary tradition, to follow the rise and decline of conventions, and to study authors and works against the background of relevant social, intellectual, political, and economic realities. A proper emphasis on literary history, however, does not mean that surveys of American and English literature should dominate the eleventh and twelfth grades. Such courses are generally too rapid and shallow to yield substantial knowledge, and when extended over a whole year, they tend to emphasize a mere bowing acquaintance with literary and cultural history at the expense of a genuine knowledge of literature itself. Bringing students to understand the significance of historical setting and sequence can often be more realistically accomplished by the study of a few major works or authors in reasonable historical depth—that is to say, by a "survey" of a few good works chronologically arranged rather than a comprehensive survey of snippets, two poems by one author, a single essay by another, and so on.

Literary Themes: The advantages of this method of setting up a course are that it demands deeper insight and more imaginative selection of material than the more arbitrary chronological survey. It appeals to the student who is concerned with ideas, and it confronts him with perennial questions and problems, allowing him to see how writers of different eras have dealt with them. This method, however, is specially susceptible to misuse and abuse. The main danger is the temptation to distort the literature to make it fit a preconceived theme. Another is to leave the literature behind for a perhaps exciting but random excursion in the regions of philosophy, psychology, social studies, and "life." Literature does indeed impinge on other disciplines and subjects, and one reason is that, as Matthew Arnold said of poetry, literature "thinks." And what it thinks about is simply everything. Nothing in human experience is alien to literature. Nor does insisting that literature is an art—and so differs from journalism, propaganda, and all sorts of utility writing—serve althogether to distinguish it from works of philosophy, science, or history such as *The Leviathan, The Golden Bough, The Origin of Species,* and *The Conquest of Mexico.* It is nonetheless a fact that literature is distinctively different from history, from anthropology, and from political theory; it is a separate form of art and must be studied in its own terms, as an imaginative construct depending for its power and persuasiveness on the deployment of language. The danger of thematic emphasis is that those peculiar terms will be obscured or obliterated, that literature will not be given a chance to appear for what it truly is.

Literary Types or Genres: The advantages of this method are that it forces the student to look upon literature as literature, not as an adjunct to philosophy, psychology, or the social studies. It invites the student to discover the variety and the range possible within each type at the same time as he becomes increasingly aware of the inescapable limitations that each form imposes upon the writer. The hazard is juiceless formalism and an excessive preoccupation with terminology and analysis. Attention to form, however, is not pointless, and usually analysis must precede integrated understanding. In fact most of what a teacher can teach and a student can learn about literature is form—the rhetorical and structural means by which literature achieves its ends. A gradually acquired and wisely used vocabulary of rhetorical and formal terms, therefore, is an essential tool in the process of analysis and synthesis, which, in turn, leads to critical understanding. If we know, for example, that "When to the sessions of sweet silent thought" begins a sonnet and a recognizable kind of sonnet, we bring to our reading of it certain expectations about its form, even about its sentiments, which are indispensable to understanding and appreciation. Knowledge of formal elements of literary work is presumably a large part of every English teacher's experience, and it is a knowledge he alone can transmit to students. Those elements do not constitute the whole of literature, but they are what distinguish it from other writing, and they must be taught if literaure is to be seriously taught at all.

These three methods of organizing the course in literature do not exclude one another. Wise teachers may well rely on no single one of these methods, seeking instead some combination that capitalizes on the advantages of each and minimizes the dangers. For such teachers some combination of literary types and literary themes may prove most practical, most exciting, and most fruitful. A class under the direction of an imaginative teacher, for instance, might explore the way the relationship between power and moral responsibility is made vivid in such a group of works as *Beowulf, Macbeth, Heart of Darkness,* and *Murder in the Cathedral.* Or they might compare and contrast the treatment of illusion in *Lord Jim* and *Death of a Salesman.* Or the part fate or destiny plays in *Oedipus, Beowulf,* and *The Return of the Native*—always, of course, with responsible awareness of just how literary form has advanced and constrained the exposition of the theme, always with close attention to the way language and structure combine to make an artistic vehicle for the theme.

The Commission is convinced that a consensus on the teaching of literature already exists and that its dwelling place is in departments of English. If that consensus is to be strengthened and clarified, teachers must welcome and exercise the responsibility for curriculum making, and colleges must improve the liberal-humanistic education of teachers of English so that an ever increasing number will be qualified, by reason of their wide and varied knowledge of both literature and criticism, for responsible and rewarding participation in the common work of their departments.

Criticism as Knowledge

One part of what the good English teacher knows, then, by wide and discriminating reading and study, is literature. But, in a perfectly practical sense, he cannot fully impart it. Only the student, by many acts of understanding and liking, can make the literature he reads his own. What can the teacher do about literature? He can talk about works expertly, ask questions about them, discuss them, think highly of them, and show his students how to think, talk, and write about what they read. Above all, he should be able to read well and, by his own example, to improve their ability to read. This is criticism, and this criticism, this process of coming to understand and evaluate, goes on as long as whatever we read continues to touch our interests and experience.

Teaching students how to look at a piece of literature, how to see what is there, how to discover what it means, and how to talk and write about what they see is a gradual process. Jerome S. Bruner's statement in *The Process of Education* applies here with particular point: "... the foundations of any subject may be taught to anybody at any age in some form." But, as Bruner also notes, "To be in command of these basic ideas, to use them effectively, requires a continual deepening of one's understanding of them that comes from learning to use them in progressively complex forms."

In the elementary grades or later, with very unsophisticated students, the teacher may do nothing but read good works aloud, interpreting them through intonation, emphasis, pacing, and a multitude of hardly noticeable indications of thought and feeling. Usually, however, the teacher as critic asks questions, primarily because criticism is a process of asking questions and attempting to answer them. Question asking is the process the students must learn, becoming critics themselves as they become increasingly adept at asking their own questions and at seeking and testing their answers. And gradually they must learn also to ask what kinds of questions they are asking, what kinds of answers they are seeking.

The criticism that results from questions asked and answered in the presence of the text (questions dealt with in this report under "The Critical Process") is not the only kind of criticism a reader makes. After the text is put aside there begins a criticism that depends on the question and answers from close reading but is substantially different. This kind of criticism is essentially comparative, and it takes two forms.

The first form occurs because, after a reader has ceased to confront the text, he can still remember it. Such remembering may be of bits and pieces, a metaphor, a character, a line. But it is also a remembering of the whole book as an intellectual and emotional experience. This recollection of the whole makes possible the comparison of one text with another or with several others. It may bring Donne's "Batter my heart, three person'd God" into comparison with Hopkins' "Thou art indeed just, Lord"—and either sonnet or both into conjunction with Eliot's "The Hollow Men." Out of this remembrance of the whole come endless possibilities for the balancings and comparisons that lead toward fuller understanding and that also lead toward comparisons of value, an important part of the act of critical judgment.

The second form of criticism that becomes possible when the text has ceased to occupy primary attention is more personal. Once the book is closed a reader no longer thinks of the text as something he can inspect, examine, probe, and dissect. Even the perfectly memorized sonnet differs from the text lying open before him. For most people the memorized sonnet is an experience of the inward eye, introspective, even auditory— a feeling that helps to define something they may ignore or deliberately suppress in the primary process of reading the open text, the realization that the literary text is never altogether "out there." Even while they are looking at it analytically, they are internalizing it, domesticating it in their own systems of thought and feeling.

When he has the text before him, a good reader makes a deliberate effort to keep intrusive thoughts and feelings out of the way of what the text is saying—a needful precaution against irrelevant associations or stock responses. But once he has read a work and closed the book, the experience begins to melt into all his other interests and feelings. Another piece of literature, a strain of music, a sudden view, a newspaper clipping, a chance meeting may remind him of it. It has become a part of him, and the questions it now evokes point toward his whole experience. This is as it should be, for when criticism is rigidly precise—when it draws back from comparison and, even more, from human experience evoked by the reading—it locks itself in a textual interior that is narrower than the consciousness of the reader. Such criticism is less than criticism.

What sets the English teacher off somewhat from the ordinary well-read man—who is certainly also a critic—is that the teacher has practiced criticism, both by reading and by writing, and has studied it both as theory and as a practice in the work of other critics. That study and practice should have given him not only a methodology but, quite as important, some freedom from a simply impulsive response. What he passes on to his students, then, is skill in putting the right questions to a text and distinguishing good answers from bad, coupled with habits of comparison and reflection that convert dead letters into live. The ultimate act of criticism is judgment. Whatever an initial response to a work of literature may be, a sound judgment of it is achievable only after the kinds of criticism briefly described above have occurred.

The Critical Process

The critical questions are, to put the matter simply, those that provoke answers essential to understanding and judging a literary work. Many of them rise quite spontaneously at first reading and are answered tentatively as they rise. The better the reader, the larger the number of questions and the quicker and surer the answers. Even for the good reader, however, there is a difference between such spontaneous questions and the ones that lead to reliable criticism: the first seek only those answers necessary for satisfying the immediate need to get from one point to another in the perusal. Questions that may be called "critical" not only reduce the tentativeness of answers but seek answers of wider import and more lasting importance. They are the questions that give direction to study after a first reading. Such questions are many, and the ones discussed below do no more than indicate kind and emphasis. The order in which they are presented, moreover, is arbitrary: the actual study of a work will determine the order in which pressing questions rise and demand answer. The Commission argues here no more than that these are fundamental questions the teacher must face as he prepares for class and then must teach his students to face as they study the work with him.

I. Questions about the text itself
    A. Questions of form
        1. What is its kind?
        2. What are its parts?
        3. How are the parts related?
    B. Questions of rhetoric
        1. Who is speaking?
        2. What is the occasion?
        3. Who is the audience?
    C. Questions about meaning
        1. What meaning has each word in its particular context?
        2. What do the diction and grammar of the text tell about its purpose?
        3. What is the paraphrasable content of the work, its "statement"?
        4. What intention—high seriousness, irony, comedy, and the like —is apparent and how is it made apparent?
        5. What part of meaning is sacrificed by paraphrase, by substitution of words other than those used by the author?
II. Questions of value
    A. Questions about personal response
    B. Questions of excellence

The first group, "Questions about the text itself," calls for answers based on textual analysis. Its first part, "Questions of form," treats the text as if it were independent of its creator and its observer. The second, "Questions of rhetoric," focuses on matters that questions of form deliberately overlook—that is, the relationship of the piece of writing to the writer or speaker, to its setting, and to its audience. The third, "Questions about meaning," runs from those about a single word to those about the work taken as a whole.

The second group, "Questions of value," is concerned with interpretation and judgment. "Questions about personal response" concern the unavoidable associations with his own experiences that arise when a reader is deeply affected by what he reads. "Questions of excellence" cover all ways of asking the final question: How good is it?

I. Questions about the Text Itself

I.A. *Questions of Form:* The questions that may be called formal are "What is its kind?" "What are its parts?" and "How are the parts related?" They are "formal" only in the sense that they ask about the form; there is nothing superficial about them. They are indeed questions natural to all learning. Since much of the process of understanding as well as of judging an object depends on comparison, a reader instinctively tries to find the class of objects with which comparison will prove most fruitful. "It looks like a poem" is the first step leading the student to subtler classification: it is a ballad, a literary ballad, a modern literary ballad. The point of such classification is not the classifying itself but the setting of expectations. The purpose is to call attention both to ballad conventions fulfilled by the particular poem and to deviations from the convention that may distinguish this poem from others of the same general type.

The second question, "What are its parts?" is also natural to the process of knowing and useful in the process of studying. The more elementary of the two ways to answer this question is to point to the places in the work where one part ends and another begins. The most useful first step is to discover into how many segments the piece can reasonably be divided—in other words, to find the largest parts first. Usually each of the main parts will consist of smaller parts. The purpose of such anatomizing is to isolate the sequential elements. In narratives of all sorts these sequential elements are episodes, or stages in the action; in arguments they are propositions or steps in the reasoning; in expositions they are successive movements of explanation. A reader must understand them individually before he looks at them in the relationships that make them parts of a whole, for the meaning of the whole will come through a series of steps in meaning, either episodic or logical. It is useless to try to build an interpretation of a work on an imperfect knowledge of what happened or of what was said.

Another way to answer the question "What are its parts?" is to consider the coordinated elements of a work rather than its sequential parts. That is, the work may be said to be made up of description, narration, exposition, or argumentation. Or it may be said to consist of characters, plot, setting, and theme. It may be said to consist of passages in elevated or low styles; or of romantic, comic, ironic, and tragic elements; or of inductive and deductive arguments; or of argument and exhortation; or of praise and blame.

The discovery and identification of parts leads to at least the beginning of an answer to the third question, "How are the parts related?" The linkage of episodes or of propositions, the logic of structure, leads to questions about the validity of the logic in an argument or exposition, or the credibility of the linkage between episodes or between motive and action. "How are the parts related?" turns out to be in part the question a reader asks spontaneously when he finishes reading the work: "Does the ending satisfy what has gone before it?"

I.B. Questions of Rhetoric: The most common rhetorical questions are: "Who is speaking?" "What is the occasion?" and "Who is the audience?"

The first of these questions is the pattern for such specific questions as "What is the character of Fra Lippo-Lippi?" or, more broadly, "Judging from this poem, what views did Robert Browning hold about life, about art?" In some works the answer may make more difference than in others, but in all it makes some difference. The question is important not only for the answer it yields but for the pressure it puts on a reader to look attentively at the language of the text, characterizing its vocabulary and syntax, noting its imagery, watching the process by which its arguments are developed.

After such attention has produced, for example, a decision about the character or the soul of Fra Lippo, the reader-critic still faces the question of who is recording or creating the monologue. Though the poet is not a speaker in this dramatic dialogue, the reader needs to know whether Lippi is a man to be believed, whether Browning uses Lippi to express his own views about life and art. In "Soliloquy of the Spanish Cloister" the issue is clearer: the savage hypocrisy of the speaker precludes admiration or even sympathy. That gives the reader a clue about the speaker behind the speaker, the poet himself; and it is a clue he may use to direct his reading of other poems by the same poet. When, in short, internal clues are not enough to provide an answer to this—or any other—critical question, the critic unhesitatingly turns to other resources. Robert Frost summed up the process in these words: "A poem is best read in the light of all the other poems ever written. We read *A* the better to read *B* (we have to start somewhere; we may get very little out of *A*). We read *B* the better to read *C, C* the better to read *D, D* the better to go back and get something more out of *A*. Progress is not the aim, but circulation. The thing is to get among the poems where they hold each other apart in their places as the stars do." (Quoted by Reuben A. Brower in *The Poetry of Robert Frost.*)

No more than the speaker in poetry does the narrator in prose fiction produce an objective report of life. No novelist can show without telling, for even an objective narrator has one or more characters through which the story must pass and by which it is given a certain form and meaning. When, therefore, a critic asks whether the narrator is telling the truth, whether he is to be believed, he is, at bottom, only asking a version of the question "Who is speaking?"

This first rhetorical question, "Who is speaking?" can, then, be answered in two different ways: dramatically and historically. The dramatic answer lies only within the piece itself, and the speaker there may be called the intrinsic speaker. The opinions or attitudes of the intrinsic speaker, Fra Lippo for example, must not be automatically identified with those of the writer—the historical, extrinsic speaker, in this case Browning. A knowledge of the author—the historical, extrinsic speaker —is always relevant to the study of a piece of writing, but it is the dramatic or intrinsic speaker who commands first and final attention.

In addition to this basic critical decision, other decisions about elements in the piece depend upon an answer to the question "Who is speaking?" These include judgments on propriety and consistency. Without a clear notion of who is speaking, there is no way to tell whether a word, a phrase, an action, or an idea is either "true to life" or consistent with the intent of the work. This kind of problem in reading, it might be noted, is at the center of a common difficulty in learning to write. Teachers of composition must constantly ask their students, "Who are you trying to make us think you are?" and "Is your voice the right one for this subject, this occasion, this audience?" In fact the most serious problems in style stem from failure to answer well the question "Who is speaking?" and to follow the principle of internal consistency.

The second question, "What is the occasion?" also refers both to a dramatic or intrinsic context and to a historical, extrinsic one. Whatever a reader can know about the occasion of Milton's writing "Lycidas," for example, supplies a historical context relevant to the study of the poem: his age and occupation at the time; his explicit ambitions and convictions; the relationship between him and Edward King, "young Lycidas"; the elegiac conventions of the time; the political-religious climate. Such knowledge is no substitute for the poem, but the poem will remain less than its full self unless such knowledge illuminates a reading of it.

Again, however, it is the intrinsic occasion, the one invented by the writer, that justifies attention to the extrinsic or historical. In some works, the ones called "occasional" because they spring from and refer directly to a particular event or experience, the question "What is the occasion?" provides no great difficulty. Wordsworth's "Lines Composed a Few Miles above Tintern Abbey, on Revisiting the Banks of the Wye During a Tour, July 13, 1798" specifies an answer in its title. Whitman's "When Lilacs Last in the Dooryard Bloom'd," Milton's *Areopagitica,* Johnson's "Letter to Lord Chesterfield": all quickly identify the events that prompted the compositions. Even with such works as Gray's "Elegy in a Country Churchyard" or Yeats' "Sailing to Byzantium," in which the occasion does not appear to have been a particular event, an occasion of some kind is implicit in the work and affects a reading of it. Part of the critic's job is to estimate—often he can do no more than that—the strength and character of the impulse behind the work. As for the question about a speaker, the answers arrived at for the second question may be tentative, but the question is justified if for no other reason than that it requires and focuses close scrutiny of the text.

The third rhetorical question, "Who is the audience?" also has two kinds of answers, historical and dramatic. Whatever a critic can find out about Shakespeare's audience, or Addison's, or Dickens', or Mark Twain's, or Tennessee Williams' may well have some bearing on an understanding of their works. The assumption, however, that every writer has a clearly defined audience in mind is treacherous. As Landor expressed it, "There is delight in singing, tho' none hear / Beside the singer." Some speakers must be thought of as speaking to the world for the sheer pleasure of speaking, or as speaking to themselves—a reminder of Yeats' remark that rhetoric is what we make when we argue with someone else and poetry is what we make when we argue with ourselves. Moreover, the distinction between public and private voice is not always easy to make—and not always very useful, once made. Yet the historical question about audience remains worth asking, for if there is an answer to it a critic may find explainable those allusions in the text that otherwise remain obscure or may measure with sounder perspective actions and arguments that appear, out of context, inappropriate.

Ultimately, however, the critic is always primarily concerned with the audience of the speaker within the work, of the intrinsic speaker and the ways in which the intrinsic, dramatic audience helps to determine the meaning of the piece. In "To His Coy Mistress" or "To an Athlete Dying Young," the answer is relatively easy. But who is the audience for the speeches beginning "Tyger! Tyger! burning bright" and "Break, break, break"—the tiger and the sea? In "Ode on a Grecian Urn," who is "ye" in "that is all / Ye know on earth, and all ye need to know"? In "The Love Song of J. Alfred Prufrock," who is "you" in "let us go then, you and I"? Who is supposed to be listening in "Ode to the West Wind," and what is the effect of speaking to things rather than to human beings? Answers to such questions are not readily come by, and sometimes unchallengeable ones cannot be made, but raising the question is itself worthwhile because it helps to focus attention on the text.

The immediacy of poems, especially of lyric poems, makes the question about audience vitally important, but it is not only for poetry that the question has relevance. In prose nonfiction, the question about audience is commonly one about the writer's assumptions and attitude. He takes much or little for granted, he concedes and qualifies frequently or not at all, he takes pains to define terms or expects his readers to proceed from a prior knowledge of them. Most authors write both for the present and for posterity and therefore generalize their audience as much as they can, but even generalizing has its limits, and it is those limits the reader must be aware of. In prose fiction the question may be all but unanswerable except in such broad forms as "written for children" or "written for those who like speculation more than action." Yet it is perfectly obvious that the audience Fielding had in mind is not the same as that Sterne or Jane Austen or Hardy set out to please and entertain. It may, of course, not even be the same for all the fiction by one author. Nonetheless, some sense of audience stimulates and guides the writer of fiction, and, however indefinite, that sense is one the reader wants to know as thoroughly as he can. If the writer does not point the way himself, the work will—by the pacing of narrative, by the amount and kind of detail, by the degree to which it is straightforward or oblique in presentation, by the language in which it is couched.

I.C. Questions about Meaning: The immediate and primary "meaning" of a literary work derives from a collection of detailed linguistic meanings involving diction, grammar, and logic. Indeed, a confident answer to the essential questions requires at least an elementary explication of the text. At first reading, for example, "Good fences make good neighbors" in Frost's "Mending Wall," seems like a simple declarative statement. On closer inquiry, however, with the total poem in mind, it opens the possibilities of irony. The Duke, in Browning's "My Last Duchess," says to the envoy "We'll go together down, sir _____," another apparently simple statement, which on close reading betrays by its emphasis on "together" something more about the character of the Duke than at first appeared. In Huck Finn's last words, "I'm going to light out for the territory," close reading is needed to estimate the implications of the word "territory" for what Huck has learned from his experiences. In Hardy's *The Return of the Native,* Mrs. Yeobright at one point pleads with her son Clym to return to Paris, where, as a jeweler, he had been doing well. Clym's reply, "Mother, what is doing well?", under this kind of scrutiny, reveals at least one other meaning for "well."

Here are examples of other questions:

A. "They hand in hand with wandring steps and slow
   Through Eden took their solitary way."
What would be the difference if you said "slow and wandering steps"?

B. "Turning and turning in the widening gyre
   The falcon cannot hear the falconer."
What do the repetitions do?

C. "I cannot praise a fugitive and cloistered virtue"
What is involved in the word "cloistered"?

D. "It is a truth universally acknowledged, that a single man in posses-
   sion of a good fortune must be in want of a wife."
How does the structure of this sentence make it comic?

E. "I should have been a pair of ragged claws
   Scuttling across the floors of silent seas."
"I should have been a————————————————"

Complete this in utterly prosaic language which says, as nearly as possible, just what the original quotation does.

Such questioning, the weighing and pondering of each word, is a proper part of careful reading. But close reading is sometimes so exhaus-
tive, and exhausting, that total meaning never emerges from it; the read-

ing becomes an exercise in ingenuity more than one in understanding. Because the danger of confusing means and end is real and serious, the importance of assessing the meaning of the whole must be stressed as one of the two major achievements of a reader.

What the questions on form and the questions on rhetoric lead up to is a sense of meaning. At the end of each set of questions, and with the help of both, a reader should be able to formulate some general statement about the intrinsic meaning of the work. This statement should be one that points into the work—that ends in the work: "'Lycidas' is a poetic lament in which the death of one young poet serves as the occasion for an interior dialogue by the speaker-poet, who in thinking about the dead poet confronts and overcomes doubts about divine providence and justice." Unsatisfactory summaries of meaning, at this level, are either mistaken—"'Lycidas' is an elegy consisting chiefly of the details of Edward King's death and funeral"—or misleading because of inadequacy —"'Lycidas' is an attack on the Church of England and an expression of Milton's egocentricity." Neither a summary statement nor a longer paraphrase is, of course, an equivalent for the work itself, but both are useful —and, in teaching, necessary—if the meaning of the whole is to be given the importance it deserves.

One problem about meaning that harasses the critic, and especially the teacher-critic, takes the form of a question about intention: "But, Miss Jones, did Shakespeare really intend to put all those meanings into his play?" In one situation, the question may be only a means of resisting instruction or of rebelling against the thought that a literary work may be more complex than the questioner is. In another, it may be serious enough to warrant attention. In both, it is inescapable. Now it may be true that, even if he tells us what his intention was, the writer's intention is unimportant except insofar as the work itself reveals it. But a surmise about the intention, as about what was not intended, may nonetheless be practically important for a reader. Common sense will tell him that the man who writes a lyric poem or a novel intended to do just that. Knowledge of matter other than the poem will tell him that Milton's "two-handed engine" passage in "Lycidas" was intended to indict the corrupt clergy and not to predict the beginning of the Revolution five years later or the death of Archbishop Laud three years later than that. Intelligent caution will keep him from concluding that, in the same poem, Milton intended by the many references to water the archetypal identification of water and womb.

There are, in short, meanings so apparent that no one can seriously doubt the writer's intention, and others less apparent but still so necessary that they have equal authority. Are there meanings, as well, that the author did not know he put into the work at all? The testimony of writers leaves no doubt that there may be, that subconsciously a work may absorb from the author ideas and feelings other than the ones he is deliberately rendering. The path from this middle ground to the rankest kind of impressionism is progressively fuller of thorns. What the work bears evidence of, even though the author may have been unconscious of putting it there, cannot be ignored; no more can it be cavalierly supplied. At this point, caution must be the watchword, caution to avoid the unlikely, the inappropriate, and the irrelevant or merely unnecessary. The aim alike in reading and in teaching should be first to discover all the meaning that is certainly there. What is done beyond that must always be tentative.

For the "beyond that" a few words will suffice. As knowledge accumulates, as perspectives change, as words change meaning, old works lose some of their immediacy, especially for young readers. The teacher may be tempted to "translate" them into familiar and contemporary idiom. If the translation is sensitively done, it may provide a temporary bridge to the original, but never more than that. The object of teaching literature is

not to bring the literature up to date but so to develop the student's ca-
pacities for understanding that he can learn to meet it on its own terms.

II. *Questions of Value*

In his inaugural lecture as professor of poetry, delivered at Oxford
University on June 11, 1956, W. H. Auden said: "Speaking for myself,
the questions which interest me most when reading a poem are two. The
first is technical. 'Here is a verbal contraption. How does it work?' The
second is, in the broadest sense, moral: 'What kind of a guy inhabits this
poem?' What is his notion of the good life or the good place? His notion
of the Evil One? What does he conceal from the reader? What does he
conceal even from himself?"

Auden's first question sounds analytical, as indeed it is, but it is evaluative, too. One can make judgments about how the poem works, after he
has analyzed carefully the technical means. He can decide that there is
too much machinery (literary technique) for the effect produced (as in
Poe's "The Raven"), or that there is not enough artistic skill to do justice
to the writer's impulse (as in most amateur verse).

The second question, in its several parts, sounds so critical that it hides
what is analytical in it. "What kind of a guy inhabits this poem?" is a
slangy and amusing way of drawing attention to the fact that all literature deals with life, in one way or another, and that the concerns one has
about life cannot be kept entirely distinct from the concerns one has
about any given work of literature.

To say "This may be a good poem, but I don't think I would like the
man who wrote it" is totally irrelevant. But it is not at all irrelevant to
ask what is the writer's conception of evil, or of good, and his awareness
of fundamental truth and falsity. It is not irrelevant to pass judgment on
these matters either, provided the judgment is not too narrow or too
superficial. Samuel Johnson regretted that Shakespeare did not always

punish the bad people and reward the good according to their deserts, but the world has come to realize that Shakespeare had a far profounder understanding of the nature of good and evil and of the way the world is than Johnson's formula could encompass.

One may argue that full answers to either the questions on form or the questions on rhetoric will yield everything that Auden seeks, just as one might argue that if he really finds out how a piece of writing works, he will know "what kind of a guy inhabits" it. Still Auden's careful distinction between "technical" and "moral" questions points to a difference about the answers that cannot be ignored. A critic can answer the technical questions quite objectively; the moral ones, no matter how objective he tries to be, will implicate responses at once less objective and more heavily weighted with emotion. If the critic detects a cynic in the authorial presence, for example, his own attitude toward cynicism will and should bear on his final judgment of the work. It will fall high or low in the absolute, though perhaps unconscious, canon by which he measures, at any given time, the things that are of value to him. When, therefore, the critic comes finally to assess the whole worth of a literary work, he inevitably finds himself employing broad moral assumptions— even if the assumption be only that, for works of literature, moral judgments are irrelevant.

In discussing questions of form and rhetoric the critic acts as though he could hold his moral and emotional response in check. He tries to consider the poem "out there"; in fact, he is probably never able to do quite that, but he is right to try. Having done so, he must still give serious attention to the event of his own reading of the work. He must ask eventually such questions as "What does it mean?" and "How good is it?"— hard questions to answer because they demand a reckoning with the whole work and the whole critic.

II.A. *Questions about Personal Response:* As he may in desperation resort to modernizing, the teacher may also find it necessary to be temporarily indulgent about private meanings, those which the student reader forwards because they satisfy some other part of his experience. And just as he moves quickly from "translation" to the original, once the purpose of the translating has been served, so he must move from the student's private meanings back toward those ascertainable from the text and from knowledge about it. Some works may indeed grow richer with the passage of time and the accretion of human experience, but the critic's goal is always to get back as close as possible to the original.

This does not imply, of course, that the reader's response to a work is unimportant, but the fact is that what a work means and what it means to him may be quite different things. He may read, or see, a play in which the leading character reminds him vividly of his father, and he may be so moved that for him this play may seem greater than *King Lear* or *Oedipus the King.* Such personal associations are inevitable at one time or other, and there is nothing wrong with them.

The question is primarily one of the relevance of the reader's reaction to a work of literary art—relevance not only to his own experience and background, but to the intrinsic qualities of the work and the general experience of mankind. Not all the student's and teacher's attention should be devoted to the formal elements of the literary work; some concern must be devoted to those social, political, or moral issues which are raised by a thoughtful reading of it.

Literature is a fine art, and its formal and artistic elements must not be neglected, but its subject matter is human. The humanity often speaks out, in a play or poem or novel, so prominently that inexperienced readers are unaware of anything else. Good teaching will make them aware of what else there is, and how important it is, without sacrificing or submerging that important human response.

Suppose a novel presents characters who are vital and convincing, a plot that is absorbing and well designed, and a style that is distinguished —but a philosophy of life the student reader finds strange and repugnant. What does the teacher do? (Many teachers find themselves in this dilemma when they are teaching Hardy's *The Return of the Native.*) The answer is not simple, and its application may be far from easy, but there are indeed ways of provoking students' imaginative participation in attitudes toward life that do not happen to be their own at the time. An extrovert girl who is bubbling over with cheerfulness may learn to participate, imaginatively, in the pathos of a Housman lyric; a cynical boy who distrusts all slogans and high-sounding language may learn to sympathize more with Hotspur than with Falstaff. The study of literature is a school for the imagination, and the imagination works as fully and creatively in the moral sphere as it does anywhere else.

Some teachers believe every reader must answer for himself this question of extrinsic meaning, of meaning beyond the work itself. They think they have done all that teachers can and should do if they have helped the student to understand the work intrinsically. The position is attractive to many for several reasons. First, it sounds professional. It identifies the attitude of the critic with that of the artist: the work speaks for itself. Second, it avoids problems about intended meanings, historical meanings, private meanings, and the meaning of meaning. Third, it nips in the bud the movement toward talk of "values" which some teachers feel is out of their reach, not part of their job, and not part of the business of any critic of art.

To be sure, the abuses of value hunting are common, commonly known, and hard to avoid. The pernicious practice of converting every literary work into a moral homily is perhaps the abuse most frequently committed. But the Commission believes that no discussion, no study, no reading of any work is complete without some consideration of possible extrinsic meaning, meaning that brings the work directly against the reader's own philosophical convictions and experience. It may be ironic that, after so many years of complaint about teachers who taught the moral instead of the work, warning should now be given against the incompleteness of any study of literature that avoids this consideration. But the Commission believes that "close reading" may as readily sterilize the study of literature as moralizing once stultified it. Perhaps the warning is needless, not just because, as Samuel Johnson said, all men are moralists, but because once men begin to ask questions, they cannot stop short of the most pressing question of all: What does this mean about life?

II.B. Questions of Excellence: Another question of value arises, the question of the value of the literary text as literature: How good is it? This question, too, has its intrinsic and extrinsic sides. The extrinsic asks whether the view of life implicit in the work is sound and whether the effects the work may have on its audience are admirable. To admit that final answers to these questions cannot be given in the classroom—or anywhere else—is not to argue that the questions should not be faced. And a negative answer is not even to argue that this work or that should or should not be taught. Almost all works worth reading seek to persuade readers to believe or do certain things and not others.

The teacher should not shirk, and the pupil should be encouraged to make, over-all evaluations of the plays, poems, novels, and essays that are studied. The method may often be that of comparison. Not all comparisons, to be sure, are useful; there is not much point in comparing chalk to cheese (for example, Clough's "Decalogue" to Shelley's "Ode to the West Wind"). But comparison carefully done makes relative worth apparent and thus helps the comparer to develop a scale of quality. Comparisons deal in such matters as appropriateness, adequacy, the adjustment of means to ends, and ultimately the importance of the subject as well as the effectiveness of the form. An example: Compare Milton's lines on Shakespeare: "What needs my Shakespeare..." with Tennyson's lines on

Milton: "O mighty-mouthed inventor of harmonies. . . ." It is not difficult to show that Milton's tribute, though extravagant in its praise, is of the most general kind, and that discrimination is sacrificed for the conceit, which draws attention to itself (and its author) rather than to any peculiar excellence in Shakespeare. Tennyson, on the other hand, has chosen to write in alcaics, a meter appropriate to a poem about the most classic of English writers. His slow, majestic rhythms suggest the opulence and solemnity of Milton's verse; and he manages to say something about Milton's achievement ("Me rather than all that bowery loneliness") which demonstrates his insight and a justness of critical judgment. For another example, compare Arnold's "To Marguerite" ("Yes: in the sea of life enisl'd") with "Dover Beach." In both, the theme is that of isolation. In the first an analogy is ingeniously and effectively worked out. Its neatness, and its exclamatory ending, can, however, best be appraised with reference to the much wider range of allusion, the larger subject, the more affecting plea ("Ah, love, let us be true to one another!") of the more famous poem. These observations lead to a consideration of the relative importance of comparable pieces of literature. Dickens' *Pickwick Papers* or H. G. Wells' *Mr. Polly,* though they are wonderfully entertaining works full of acute observation, may be called lesser achievements than *Middlemarch* or *Sons and Lovers* simply because they do not touch on so many of the important problems of life, or probe so profoundly the issues with which we are faced.

The pupil will discover that generally speaking the great writers develop systems, patterns they discern in human experience, which constitute a kind of philosophy. It is one of the obligations of the serious reader to put together the author's system, to test its completeness, and to try its strength by poising his own experience against it. But here the reader must beware lest he dismiss without careful examination an unfamiliar criticism of life as irrelevant and inadequate. Like a traveler in a foreign country, he carries his prejudices with him when he ventures into areas of literature that lie somewhat remote from his own time and place. He must expect to acclimatize himself, and like the traveler try to understand the whole pattern of his new environment. It is only in this way that he can enlarge his views, lose his parochialism, and achieve the end toward which humane education directs him—that is, he will become not only better informed, but also tempered by his assimilation of some, at least, of the best that has been said and thought. Much of the teacher's responsibility is to act as *cicerone* in this foreign territory.

But the intrinsic version of the question of excellence is the one we wish to end with: How good is it? Even with his relatively limited background, the student can make a start toward answering this question. An answer requires that he consider the extent to which a given work furnishes interesting answers to all the other essential questions we have been discussing, answers that suggest a conscious and subtle harmony and interplay of elements. He will then soon discover why *Macbeth* is a better play than *Cat on a Hot Tin Roof*. And he will come to recognize why *The Return of the Native* stands up for hours under the kind of literary scrutiny that makes short work of *Gone with the Wind*. He will not—nor will his teacher—by these discoveries establish a ladder of excellence beyond dispute, but he will learn to discriminate on reliable grounds, and he will learn to respect the act of discrimination.

These, then, are some of the important questions that the teacher asks as he prepares for class and that he will teach students to ask as they read. Though they are presented schematically here, in practice they will arise as the text itself suggests them, some more insistently than others but all with sufficient frequency to make bearing them in mind a means of assuring close and thoughtful attention during study.

Questions for Learning, Teaching, and Testing

The foregoing discussion of "critical questions" about literature suggests, as it is meant to do, that the process of questioning is essential to critical activity. It represents not only a procedure but an attitude, and the attitude is one that the Commission believes should dominate the English classroom in secondary school whenever literature is being read or taught. The spirit of inquiry, the belief that answers are worth working for, and the willingness to accept answers that are less than final and absolute: these characterize the attitude most likely to make the study of literature worthwhile, especially for the adolescent, to whom questions and the effort to answer them are almost a way of life.

Three kinds of questions are distinguishable in this teaching-learning situation: those the teacher asks as he prepares his lessons, those he asks in the actual teaching of it, and those he asks when the teaching is over —learning questions, teaching questions, and testing questions. All three have the same ultimate object, but their strategy will often be quite different.

The learning questions are those the teacher asks before he knows the answers, and he asks them of himself as a way of coming to understand the work he is to teach. Essentially, they stimulate him to learn everything he needs to know about the work before he decides how to teach it, and they must therefore cover, in whatever order is natural at the time of preparation, all the matters discussed in the preceding section, matters of form, rhetoric, meaning, and value. These are also the questions the teacher wants his students to learn how to ask and to ask systematically on their own. But teaching them to do so is not simply a matter of repeating aloud the questions privately asked in the process of preparation.

The difference between learning questions and teaching questions may be put in this way: the former lead to answers the teacher does not know until he has puzzled them out, the latter to answers the teacher already knows but his students do not, or do not yet know they know. The teaching questions, then, are essentially Socratic, a means not of discovering the unknown but of communicating the known. Plato always represents Socrates as having what the teacher must have—confidence in his own superior though not perfect knowledge. The Socratic question is always one of a series of questions, each of which, however casual it appears, is based on some step just made and is designed to produce another step, the total series leading ultimately to a predetermined conclusion—in an English class, to the fullest understanding that the teacher can achieve of the text under discussion. A teacher using this method does not ask questions at random or questions that lead nowhere. He must have a clear idea before he begins the steps by which he plans to proceed, and he must know beforehand the answers (there may be more than one to each question, of course) that make the next questions relevant.

Ideally, the teaching questions begin either with the issue on which interest is likely to be highest and answers most varied and assertive, or at a point of decision on which most other decisions about the text will depend. In the study of Thornton Wilder's *The Bridge of San Luis Rey,* for example, the teaching questions might start with titles. Why does Wilder call the first part "Perhaps an Accident," and the last part "Perhaps an Intention"? Why are the intervening parts named for three particular people: The Marquesa de Montemayor, Esteban, and Uncle Pio? Why is none of them named for the Abbess, an important figure in the book and, as history is to know her, "one of the two great women of Peru"? Answers to these questions, basically about meaning, open the way for others of different kind, those leading perhaps in the end to the "formal" question from which the teacher may have started his own inquiry: "Is this really a novel at all or only a collection of stories about a group of people whose lives are connected?" The point to be made about teaching questions is simply that they must be so carefully planned that, even when answers lead off in many directions, those most likely to produce a thorough exploration will be the ones seized as ground for the next step.

Since the purpose of the teaching questions is to put the student in the way of learning to ask questions by himself, they should be followed by a careful summary that makes clear what has been learned in the process of finding answers to them. From each study of a text students should emerge progressively more sure of what they need to know about a work to know it well.

The ideal testing question should fully reveal what a student knows about something and provoke answers that can be reliably evaluated; its prototype is the objective, machine-scorable question common to all national testing programs. In such programs it can be justified on grounds of efficiency and reliability of measurement; in the local classroom neither is at such premium as to warrant its exclusive use. The defects of objective questions, particularly for subjects like English and history, are two, and both are serious ones. In the first place, the most interesting, searching, and significant questions often call for answers that cannot be popped into a scoring machine: To what extent could it be said that Brutus is the villain rather than the hero of *Julius Caesar*? What is the significance of Jody's losing interest in the mouse hunt in *The Leader of the People*? In the second place, objective questions, except when most expertly designed, fail to achieve the full purposes of a good examination. Teaching questions test as they teach, and testing questions—at least, some of them—should teach as they test. That is, though testing questions are properly intended to find out what a student knows, they should at the same time stimulate him to use what he knows in new ways. It is important to find out how much a student knows about a work he has studied, but it is also important to find out how much that knowledge has increased his ability to respond intelligently to literature in general. When both values are respected, a good test will call for precision but will simultaneously require more than mere memory and the recitation of answers already learned.

Taken together, the three kinds of questions provide the kind of full inquiry that makes the study of literature not a chore but a serious venture in education. They do not preclude lecturing, but they do subordinate it, for the main goal in secondary school teaching should be not simply to stock the mind with matter but to strengthen and discipline it while it is being stocked.

Composition

The ablest student answers in the Commission's *End-of-Year Examinations in English for College-Bound Students, Grades 9-12* offer an impressive rejoinder to the perennial lament that students can't write and that English teachers either can't or don't teach writing. Obviously some students can write—possibly better than their parents or grandparents did at the same age. And these students write well at least partly because they have been ably taught. This is not to say that all is well with the teaching of composition in the secondary schools. Far from it! But there are clear signs that it is far from being the total failure it is said to be: first, the actual writing of the ablest and best trained secondary school students; second, the discontent among English teachers themselves with the present state of composition; and third, the eagerness teachers show about learning to do better what many regard as the toughest but most important part of their jobs, and the part for which their college training has least well prepared them.

Two Views of Composition

The Student's View

Since the teaching of literature takes its point of departure from the text itself, it is appropriate that discussion of it should also begin from the text. In the teaching of composition, however, there is no text to begin from; the point of departure for it is properly the student about to compose a text. For him, and for the person who is to teach him, the difference is crucial. It is not just that analysis is different from synthesis, or that learning how to see and to understand is different from learning how to show and to communicate. The difference goes deeper, to the very quick of the student's life, where, like any writer, he exposes himself to public scrutiny, lays his mind bare for all to see.

In 1644, when John Milton was "assigned" an essay on education, he said that he thought it was a mistake to force young people to write before they had anything to say or a desire to say it. A counsel of perfection, no doubt, but one that no teacher of composition can ignore, for in the long run no composition has much value in the process of education except composition stemming from readiness to say something. Yet it is precisely when he does have something to say and the desire to say it that the student feels himself most vulnerable, most open to attack, and most sensitive about what he has said.

Caught between reluctance to expose himself and indifference to subjects on which he really does not have anything he wants very much to say, the student may reasonably be inclined to argue that composition is a waste of time. He can point out that, whatever they say to the contrary, men rise to the top in commerce and industry who express themselves almost entirely by spoken words or in the limited written language of a science or a technology; that it is perfectly possible to achieve high places in political and even diplomatic life without writing anything more complicated than factual reports (a skill not to be taken lightly but one that does not impress the adolescent as particularly taxing). He is likely to know, moreover, that most prominent and busy men have "writers" who compose for them, and he may even consider the plagiarizing of printed matter or of another student's essay not much different from reading aloud in public as one's own what someone else has actually written. He knows certainly that the world's business in these days is done largely by telephones and tape recorders, in conversations and conferences, in dictated memorandums and directives.

It cannot be denied that the student's view of composition is affected by his awareness that speech will play a much larger part than writing in his life. And his attitude toward writing is also affected by this fact in another way. He senses a disparity between the language and syntax of written composition and that of even good oral composition—a disparity that extends from organization to usage—and he does not know, unless he is taught, how to deal with it. Here the help of a well-informed teacher is of great importance. If the teacher knows enough about language to recognize that it changes and how it changes, he can show students that appropriateness is a more helpful canon than prescribed and inflexible forms (a matter discussed in this report under "Language"). He will become and teach his students to become judicious arbiters rather than unthinking imitators of inherited patterns. Unless he does so, students will be increasingly frustrated by the difference between what experience teaches them about language and what outdated textbooks tell them is correct.

In the end, however, the most serious difficulty students face in composition, whether they can articulate it or not, is the one mentioned at the beginning: for them, writing a composition is always a kind of test, laying it on the line, and for many reasons that challenge is not always welcome. English composition is for them what writing, serious writing, is for everyone—a revelation over which the writer knows he does not have perfect control. He cannot help giving himself away to the eyes of an alert reader, and many students must, in a way, resent this forced self-revelation.

Yet the fact remains that students do produce essays generated by the passion for an idea and a passion to teach, persuade, or please others with that idea. That they do and can is assurance that the teaching of composition is neither a hopeless chore nor a futile one.

Emphasis is placed here on written composition, but nothing in this report should be construed as denying the importance of instruction in spoken English. The Commission believes that what is most important in speaking is also most important in writing—thought and its expression—and the discussion that follows is as relevant to the one as to the other. The Commission's concern is not with courses in remedial speech or in public speaking; it is rather with the ability of the student to make himself audible, intelligible, and persuasive when he participates in discussion or stands before the class to speak. To enunciate clearly, to control inflection, to stand and move gracefully, to sense and respond to the reaction of an audience: these minimal techniques can and should be taught, and the place to teach them is everywhere that speaking occurs. That is to say, teachers of English and of other subjects should require that all spoken performance in the classroom be the subject of instruction. Teachers, especially English teachers, have as much obligation to develop clear, succinct, and fluent speech in recitations as to develop good writing. The example set by the teacher is of first importance.

The Teacher's View

A good English teacher sees the subject and the activity of composition not only sympathetically from the student's point of view, but also professionally from prospects peculiarly his own, some new and some traditional. Our times are still influenced by the intellectual revolution that began in the Renaissance as well as by many concepts of the Greek-Christian metaphysics. But in the 1960's a whole generation of teachers must have somewhat different attitudes toward knowledge and truth than did teachers of 50, even 25 years ago, and somewhat different concepts of the answerable questions as well as of the acceptable answers and the processes proper for finding them. More and more, English teachers will be people whose ideas about composition, logic, and style show the influence of philosophy developed from the logical positivists, from existentialism and pragmatism, from scientific thought, even from the new mathematics; and of a taste that has been subtly but deeply affected by contemporary writers from Joyce and Pound to Camus and Albee. In fact, many among the younger English teachers must now often be disturbed by the inconsistency between the liberalism of their convictions about music, painting, and philosophy, and the conservatism and conventionality of the doctrine and taste they may be teaching in English composition.

It is true, of course, that from the beginning, teachers of rhetoric have known and taught that usage is a relative, not an absolute, matter—that what was correct depended upon the time, the place, the subject, the audience, and the speaker. And the best teachers of English, from the seventeenth-century critics on, have recognized that language and taste change—from time to time, from place to place, from person to person. But in our own time the awareness that language operates on a scale of relativity is so widely admitted, in practice even when not in theory, that a teacher of composition must often feel that he has nothing but shifting sands under his feet.

The result is that an English teacher today, confronting a student's composition, may feel more alone, more on his own, than did teachers 50 years ago. Certainly he never has been more on his own. He knows that in correcting a paper he is testing himself as teachers in earlier days did not. He cannot justify his corrections by reference to rules alone, and often he cannot prove he is right simply by reference to a dictionary. He must fit himself to be more than a proofreader, to become something closer to an expert and sympathetic editor.

None of the frustrations, however, none of the buffetings English teachers suffer from uncertainties about what is true, whether it can be found, whether it can be experienced—about what is correct or what is in good taste—about what is beautiful or good—none of these difficulties is any greater than those introduced into the task by the human factor, by the complexities of the student, the young writer. A good teacher knows that the acquisition of skill in writing is gradual, and that it is inseparable from the processes of physical, social, emotional, moral, and intellectual growth. That is the same as saying he knows that much of what is wrong (or right) with a student's writing is what is wrong (or right) with the student, or with his parents, or with his culture, or (if the teacher is honest) with the teacher himself. Composition is a revealing business. Even an essay entitled "How the Student Council Is Elected" or "How Plattsburg Was Founded" may reveal enough to make the English teacher wiser about the mind and heart of his students than the teacher of any other subject.

Part of the success of a good teacher of composition, then, comes from charity rooted in his awareness of the common weakness and strength of humanity. What makes him able to help students write better may be largely his sympathy with anyone who is struggling to order his experience and who, in the simultaneous ordering and expressing of that experience, hopes to acquit himself well—to create something pleasing, instructive, or persuasive—or perhaps just to enjoy the human feeling that other human beings understand him and approve.

Like life itself, all writing is concerned with truth. For despite all the difficulties about truth that students and teachers must share, English teachers must not make the mistake of thinking that true and false are meaningless terms for composition. They must, instead, make it always clear that in whatever other ways writing may be faulty, it must not be and need not be false. To pretend to care, to pretend to believe, to pretend to know, and to pretend to be are the most common violations of truth in student writing. To say as much is not to deny the difference between the real author and the voice of the speaker, or speakers, in any piece of writing, fiction or nonfiction. Nor is it to deny the natural and, in some ways, admirable desire of all men to present themselves as better than they are. It is not a denial of art or of the need for masks through which to speak. It is rather a recognition of the dangers of forcing people to write and then, by the threat of criticism, forcing them to say or feel or be what they are not. It is a recognition that to learn to write well one must care—care for the truth, care for the audience, care for one's own integrity.

Of course, teachers must know that much falseness in writing comes from self-deception, and no good teacher can avoid being Socratic to the extent of making his students aware that it is desirable, though difficult, to know themselves. At times English teachers may find it hard to draw the necessary line between teacher of composition and lay analyst, because it is sometimes hard to show why the tone of voice in a piece of writing is false without assuming to know something about the character of the writer. What is known, or thought to be known, may be what the writer did not know; simply as critic of the writing, the teacher must be able to describe the character of the voice of the paper, and thus let the writer decide whether that is either his own character or the character he wishes to assume.

Other forms of falseness are no less frequent than that of self-deception. It is hard, but essential, to teach young writers the difference between what they really know and what someone else may have said—to show them why they may say, "This is the best story of Hemingway we have read," or "This is Hemingway's last published story," but may not say, "This is Hemingway's finest story," unless they have read them all, or "This story brought to a close a chapter in American literary history," no matter how many stories they have read. Finally, teachers can and must show why arguing for unexamined opinions is a form of pretension because the self-deception involved, whatever the opinions expressed, will make the essay false in feeling if not in fact.

If a teacher can convince his students that he expects the best, the truest account, explanation, or argument they can discover, and if he can inspire in his students the ambition, courage, and energy to stop being insensitive, unperceptive, and superficial, his good fortune will be to watch his young writers develop in power and grace. This is a tall order, but its size is proportionate to the one acceptable goal, that of teaching students above all to be honest in their writing. How teachers induce these necessary attitudes is harder to say. Their own rhetoric must, of course, be honest, and its honesty will depend on their caring, on their being as true to their own experience as they can be, on their rejection of the temptations to be phony, cynical, or trivial. It will also depend on their wisdom and skill—how much they know, how much they themselves write.

In the end, no one persuades well without being able to convince his hearers of the rewards available to those who will agree or follow. In composition, two of the rewards, two of the joys, are delight in discovery that comes as one writes and the sense of power that accompanies the sense of achievement. A good teacher shares the delight of his students and expresses pleasure in their discoveries. And he treats their papers as if they were works of art, the offspring of the writers, little pieces of themselves. A good teacher knows, or is constantly reminded, that he doesn't do much except preside at the birth or provide a place or occasion for the conception. He knows, indeed, that, as one master teacher has said, teachers more than anyone else except a parent must bide their time and live in the midst of uncertainties, expressing the virtue which Keats calls "negative capability" without "irritable reaching after fact and reason."

Organizing Instruction in Writing

At the beginning of his seminal work on rhetoric, Aristotle reminded his students that in the making of any discourse they would consider three elements: the speaker or writer; the audience; and the subject. This simple sounding statement has led critics to useful lines of inquiry, especially as they have focused on one or another of the elements.

When the critic, the rhetorician, or the teacher focuses on the third of Aristotle's elements—presentation of the subject in a speech or composition or work of literary art—his emphasis is on questions of form: What kind is it? What are its parts? How are they related? And though the answers to these questions lead to a consideration of both the writer and the reader, still the emphasis is on the work of art, the thing itself; and a theory of poetry or of speaking or of composition formed with this emphasis and focus will tend toward more precision, more "rules" or "laws," than will a theory that emphasizes or focuses on either the writer or the reader.

When the critic centers his study in the reader or audience, his questions will be more concerned with rhetoric than with form: Who is being addressed? What is the occasion? Are the occasion and the voice appropriate to the audience? What effect was intended—or produced? The difference between a "formal" approach and a "rhetorical" approach is, at bottom, only one of emphasis. And although the discoveries made by the two emphases are themselves different, the methods themselves are not mutually exclusive but complementary. The teacher cannot say that one is essentially better than the other, though either one is the better for incorporating as much of the other as possible.

Now what of a critical approach that focuses on the first of Aristotle's triad—the speaker or the writer? In the earlier discussion of critical questions no separate class derived from a focus on the writer, but there the concern was primarily with literature. The study of literature should begin and end with the work itself, whereas in composition, it may be argued, one should begin at the beginning—that is, with the writer. How to begin with the writer requires some speculation about what student writers are like, how their minds work, how their emotions affect them in various states of their development.

One of the currently popular theories about education (the spiral curriculum) seems to be indebted to Alfred North Whitehead. In a lecture titled "The Rhythm of Education"—published in *The Aims of Education*—Whitehead discusses learning as a cyclic process consisting of three stages: the stage of romance, the stage of precision, and the stage of generalization. The total education of a man, he argues, consists of cycles within cycles or cycles of cycles.

"The whole period of growth from infancy to manhood forms one grand cycle. Its stage of romance stretches across the first dozen years of life, its stage of precision comprises the whole school period of secondary education, and its stage of generalization is the period of entrance into manhood. . . . The university course or its equivalent is the great period of generalization."

Whitehead describes the stage of romance as follows:

"The stage of romance is the stage of first apprehension. The subject-matter has the vividness of novelty; it holds within itself unexplored connections with possibilities half disclosed by glimpses and half concealed by the wealth of material. In this stage knowledge is not dominated by systematic procedure. Such system as there must be is created piecemeal ad hoc. We are in the presence of immediate cognizance of fact, only intermittently subjecting fact to systematic dissection. Romantic emotion is essentially the excitement consequent on the transition from the base facts to the first realizations of the import of their unexplored relationships."

This large concept may serve the composition teacher as a kind of principle for certain useful beginning exercises in writing—exercises in which the writer is given the freedom he needs to make those discoveries about himself and the world that Whitehead calls characteristic of the stage of romance. In fact, in another essay in *The Aims of Education,* "The Rhythmic Claims of Freedom and Discipline," Whitehead calls this first stage the stage of freedom and discusses its uses in terms of special interest to teachers of composition. At some time, early in the life of the student and early in each of the succeeding stages—that is, in the early grades, and early in every grade—the teacher must try to reach the student's inmost interests and real thoughts. At this point he must be something of a friendly enemy, a confessor, a deeply attentive listener, a dramatist of the student's imagination. He must learn to recognize what a student is seeking and learn how to make assignments that lead sometimes not to "compositions" but to discoveries of perception and emotion out of which writing may come later—in other years, perhaps—and without which writing remains only a practical operation, like putting up smoke signals or running an automatic elevator. If the study of literature is a source of civilized joy and a human discipline, the same should be true of the art of writing. Not every reader, though well taught, will be a good reader; and the same holds for the writer, but the chance to learn these pleasures and absorb these values is a function of freedom— the freedom which is characteristic of the stage of romance.

This is enough to suggest further implications of Whitehead's theory of cycles. In composition the early years might concentrate on what, in the best sense, is creative writing—not writing aimed to create artistic forms or works of art, but writing aimed primarily at expression, at discovery of the self and the world. The next stage might concentrate on the discipline of form—on those matters of arrangement, logic, and conventional correctness that make up the body of most books on composition. And in the third stage, which in Whitehead's cycle is a return to freedom, teachers might promote the comprehensive view of composition which combines the pleasure and freedom of the first with the instruction and discipline of the second. This third stage should witness the development of style, as the first stage witnesses the development of invention, and the second of methods of arrangement and form. To quote Whitehead again (from his first essay in *The Aims of Education*):

"Finally, there should grow the most austere of all mental qualities; I mean the sense for style. It is an aesthetic sense, based on admiration for the direct attainment of a foreseen end, simply and without waste. Style in art, style in literature, style in science, style in logic, style in practical execution have fundamentally the same aesthetic qualities, namely attainment and restraint.... Style, in its finest sense, is the last acquirement of the educated mind; it is also the most useful. It pervades the whole being. The administrator with a sense for style hates waste; ... the artisan with a sense for style prefers good work. Style is the ultimate morality of mind."

These three "stages" in the teaching of composition are not, however, simply the stages of junior high, senior high, and college, though they are that in part. They are the stages of every cycle of instruction in composition. In every year—in ninth grade English, in eleventh grade English, in college freshman English—teachers may experience the same cycle of freedom, discipline, and freedom—with the final freedom vastly different from the initial one. The application of spiraling movement to instruction in writing has proved, in good hands, effective enough to warrant recommendation as the vital principle for organizing instruction in writing.

However well he organizes his instruction, however well he teaches, the English teacher must content himself with less than measurable certainty about the outcome of his work.

The task is complicated, and the possibilities of change are limited. Before a student gets to secondary school his heredity, his environment, and his early education have determined most of what we call intelligence and verbal aptitude. The distance he has already traveled is so great compared with the distance of the course he will run in English that changes in velocity and direction are likely to be minor. In an age that demands measurement and pays most for what can be measured, the English teacher may often be frustrated by the fact that he cannot easily measure the progress he may have helped his students to make.

What keeps him on the job is partly his pleasure in a sense of life and partly his conviction about the value of the civilization that the humane activity of writing helps to maintain, no matter how unmeasurable this pleasure and this conviction may be. When he admits that he cannot precisely measure such qualities of the good writer as understanding of his own and other people's feelings, power of making experience and observations clear and alive, power of making thoughts persuasive, or love of truth, the teacher of composition still does not admit that the subject called English is meaningless. He merely accepts what literature and the other arts rejoice to affirm: the things men value most cannot be measured.

Composition Assignments

No part of an English teacher's job is more important or more a test of his mettle than the making of sound, well-framed assignments, what is above called "providing the occasion." The assignments must be difficult enough to make the student reach higher than he thought he could and stimulating enough to make him want to write. Haphazard assignments, flung out as the bell rings, are an invitation to false and superficial response. Making good ones is an art, and the art has principles that can be quite specifically stated. Designing them takes more time and more imagination than most teachers give to it, but if the teacher thinks of it as the heart of his teaching—in short, if he thinks that what he asks of his students is more important than what he tells them—he may be ready to spend almost as much time, energy, and imagination on creating the assignments (and even writing out answers to them) as on reading the papers that result.

A good assignment evokes the best from the writer and gives the teacher the best chance to be helpful. It asks the student to do something he can almost, but not quite, do without strain. It asks for nothing that the teacher cannot, with effort, understand well enough to criticize intelligently, both in form and in content. The vacuous subject, "What I did on my summer vacation," fails because the poorest student learns little from treating it, and the best finds in it no stretch for the mind. The recondite one, "Gamma particles under pressure," fails because, unless the teacher knows at least as much about the subject as the writer, it gives him no opportunity to serve the student as more than a proofreader. He may think that he can judge the essay by its success in making unknown matter clear to him, but in fact he has no way of knowing that it is clear unless he also knows that it is accurate.

A good assignment aids learning and requires a response that is the product of discovery. The lackluster writer is primarily one who has not discovered anything worth saying. The writer must care. The reader must be made to care in some way if he is to make useful comments about the theme, and no reader can care if he feels the writer did not care in the first place. The assignment must therefore touch the outer edge of the student's knowledge and invite him to go further, and it must guarantee that going further will give him the chance of discovering something he did not know before.

To provide that invitation and guarantee that discovery, *a good assignment furnishes data to start from.* "Let us assume . . . ," it begins; or "Assuming the following things to be true, write...." It may set conflicting data, such as contradictory criticism of a literary text, opposing arguments, incongruous bits of common sense ("A penny saved is a penny earned" and "Penny wise, pound foolish"). It may start from a picture or even from a cartoon, like the now famous one that appeared originally in *The New Yorker* several years back showing a child at the dinner table who, when her mother says, "It's broccoli, dear," replies, "I say it's spinach, and I say the hell with it," a cartoon that poses the same question as that raised by Juliet's confidence that a rose by any other name would smell as sweet. For college preparatory students especially, the data should often be the literature they are studying, an endless source for good subjects which has the advantage of providing its own data.

A good assignment may take the form of, or be construable into, a proposition. The conversion of a theme "topic" into a proposition is helpful because it gives students something definite to work against. "The view from my window" has the virtue of inviting invention but the serious fault of giving the writer nothing to control his attention. Translated to propositional form—"That the view from my window makes me dread (or welcome) getting up in the morning"—the same topic suggests a focus and even a tone for the writer to exploit. The literary essay benefits no less from a propositional starting point: "That Hamlet is mad," "That Macbeth is a responsible agent," "That Lanier's poetry is more sound than sense." Obviously, it is not necessary that the assignment be couched in such formal terms, but it is important that the student be taught to see that, however it is couched, it contains a central proposition, or more than one, and that propositions require more than sentiment from him. The provision of a predicate immediately puts the writer into a posture of defense or attack and calls for the summoning and ordering of evidence or arguments. Instead of a circle circumscribing undefined matter, the proposition supplies an arrow pointing out a clear direction of movement.

A good assignment limits either form or content or both. By limitation the teacher reduces the choices that a writer must make. He stakes out the limits within which the writer may exercise his freedom and thus makes it possible for him to compare results; for, though no two good themes will be alike, they must have similarities if the teacher is to practice on them, for the benefit of the class, that most useful of critical procedures, comparison. It is for the same reason that he furnishes certain data, certain givens. He wants not only to stimulate good writing but to make use of it after it is written. When he reads the papers he will, to be sure, consider not only the satisfactoriness with which the limited element is managed but the ingenuity the student has shown in managing what was left free. And when he uses the papers for class discussion he will do no less.

Wherever feasible, a good assignment will stipulate the audience to be addressed. Too many English themes seem addressed either to the teacher (who is unlikely to be such a stuffed shirt as the style of the paper often implies) or, in a vague romantic way, to the world or posterity or some Saroyanesque "You Out There." Some assignments, it is true, may have a very general audience; for the novice especially, it may be inhibiting rather than helpful to require that he think of a specific audience for a poem or for any of the range of forms that are more "literary" than expository or argumentative. And some assignments— summaries and paraphrases and precis in particular—have an audience too obvious to need much emphasis; it is simply the teacher, who wants to make sure a text has been carefully read, or the class, which can get from it information about something it has not read. Most themes, however, have neither so definite nor so large an audience. Their true audience is one in the student's mind, and his writing will be sharpened in proportion to his awareness of the demands that audience makes on him.

To inculcate the habit of considering audience, the teacher may vary the stipulations and begin with fairly simple exercises: "Write a letter to the governor arguing that . . . ," "Write a petition to the student council or the principal requesting that . . . ," "Write an essay on the proposition that . . . , for submission to *The Reader's Digest,* to *Life,* to *Harper's,* to *Field and Stream.*" As his sense of audience is sharpened, as the matter of appropriate style and content becomes clear to him, the student should be more and more frequently expected to define his own audience and eventually to define it, not in so many words, but by tone and content alone. As a practical matter, he should find his own class the most suitable audience because the class doesn't have to be imagined, though it does have to be observed. Its membership is various enough to make his job hard and yet homogeneous enough to limit the difficulty. Best of all, the class is right there. Both teacher and student can consult it when the theme is written. The writer does not need to guess what the reaction might be; he can find out.

Assignments should vary in kind. The Commission believes that there is no sacred pattern of progression, from description through narration to argument, for instance, nor any from matters of daily living to outpourings of the heart or ruminations of the spirit. The precis, the summary, the parody, the imitation of a master are all valuable exercises. The mere process of trying to write poems or stories sharpens the student's appreciation of the poetry and fiction he is studying and leaves him respectfully aware of the masterly technique required to make a poem or story sound so effortless that you think what it tells must just have happened that way. In making such assignments, a good teacher will in his own mind, however, stress the value of the process more than the worth of the product. Both the formal exercise and the creative effort yield much that is valuable, but for most students neither does as much as expository writing, broadly defined, to arouse curiosity, stimulate the pleasure of discovery, or inculcate the love of truth. During the eleventh and twelfth grades, at least, the expository essay should be the staple of the course. It best serves the other parts of the student's education; it prepares him best for the writing he will do in college; it allows the best definition of problems and permits the most helpful exercise of informed criticism by the teacher; it provides the best classroom exercise because its discipline is the best understood; and it is, in however corrupted condition, the most common form of human discourse.

But there is more to giving theme assignments than the finding of sound, provocative topics. The presentation is as important as the finding. If a teacher wants to incite healthy grapplings with significant questions, he will take time in class to discuss purposes and clarify directions and so arouse the highest possible interest. He will forestall needless difficulties by anticipating them. Suppose a teacher asks his tenth grade students to write a composition in which they compare and contrast the two candidates for president of the school government. Obviously organization will be a major issue in any kind of comparative essay, and unless the teacher spends a good part of the period demonstrating different ways of setting up a comparative organization, what his students will give him will be a first section on the first candidate followed by a second section on the second candidate probably introduced with a "Now let us turn to" and then a third section of perfunctory summation ushered in with a "Thus I have shown." The teacher's job in making the assignment is to convince his students that alternative plans are possible, such as comparing the two candidates, point by point, under headings like: previous evidence of responsible leadership; previous evidence of ability to speak effectively in public; previous evidence of ability to handle the academic work quickly and effectively; previous evidence of wisely selected extracurricular interests; previous evidence of ability to get on with all kinds of people.

A teacher of English composition should take theme assignment seriously, and by the care with which it is planned and the deliberateness, clarity, and imagination with which it is presented he should make clear to the class that if they will take the assignment seriously (even the spinach-broccoli cartoon), the teacher and the rest of the audience—the class—will take their essays seriously. Composition teachers who think of an assignment as simply a way of getting a piece of writing to correct defeat their own purposes, for how can students take substance seriously if they suspect the teacher doesn't? And why should students respect teachers who call for a paper the student can't read to the class without either embarrassment or the smirk which implies that he thinks his classmates share his contempt for the whole business? It is not just a matter of assigning hard topics. It is rather a matter of not doing anything in a course in English that is trivial or simply routine. Not that every assignment should come wrapped in owlish solemnity. No one, least of all the English teacher, wants to take the joy out of creation or the smile out of the human condition. The plea here is only that college-bound students be exercised in writing disciplined essays on ideas—though these ideas may be no more solemn than those expressed or latent in the broccoli cartoon.

Correction, Criticism, and Measurement

Making a good theme assignment may take several hours; reading the themes from each class as they should be read is sure to do so, but the instruction such a reading provides is ample warrant for the time necessary to do a good job of it. In the nature of things, the teacher is part of the audience for the paper. If he has taught his class to direct the writing toward their peers, or another group, for that matter, his first act must be that of empathy—that is, he must become part of that audience as he reads. At the same time, he must exercise his function as teacher, which is to say as expert reader and editor, so that what he says about the paper will not be its epitaph but a prelude to further learning.

Even the most cursory reading should be accompanied by the marking of errors in spelling, punctuation, grammar, and diction. Sometimes corrections should be supplied, more often only the need for them indicated wherever faults occur that the student will be required to correct. "Correction" and "correctness" suffer some obloquy today, and on the whole it has been good for English teachers to be reminded that the word "correct" may often mean only "appropriate," and that something can be appropriate only in relation to something else, to a context. Violations of linguistic decorum are not violations of statute but only of conventions prevailing in certain situations. At the same time, the admission that usage is relative exacts more, not less, discipline from the writer, and the teacher must be constantly alert to indict and require correction of faults in form and failures of taste.

Though necessary, this activity is minimal. Ideally the teacher should not only read every paper and mark its formal errors but should write detailed comment. The comment need not be complete for each paper read, but it should always be constructive and specific, showing the student exactly what might be done to improve the theme and what has been successfully done in the theme as presented. In the course of a year, the comment should make as coherent a progress as the classroom teaching, directing each writer to examine and correct his worst faults one by one, so that at the end of the year he can look back on measurable improvement. (Since each student will present different major faults, the teacher should keep a journal in which to record, after each theme is corrected, the points he has emphasized as needing particular attention; then he, too, can calculate the progress of each writer and check the sequence of his own instruction.) And, ideally, after each paper is returned, the teacher should confer with its writer to make sure that corrections have been made and that the terminal comment is understood.

For most teachers, however, the ideal kind of reading and correction is out of the question. Even for 100 students (the present average is closer to 150), individual conferences take more time than any teacher has, a thoughtful written comment on each paper is an impossibility, and even a rapid reading is a severe tax on energy and endurance. Yet somehow the job must get done, and substitute procedures therefore deserve attention:

The "lay reader." In recent years many schools have provided help for the English teacher by hiring well-educated people in the community to assist in reading and commenting on themes and in conferring with students about them. The lay reader should attend the class in which the assignment is given, and he must work closely enough with the teacher to make sure that his commentary is a genuine aid. The teacher himself reads some of the themes carefully and may want to read all of them rapidly, either before or after the lay reader has worked on them. Experience with this plan shows that it has the advantage, not so much of saving a great amount of the teacher's time as of giving students more assistance and often a second reader for their work.

Topical commentary. Lacking time for discursive comment, a teacher may take his cue from readers of national examinations and supply, in place of comment, a grade (number, letter, or single word) for each of the principal topics of ordinary correction: writing skills (spelling, punctuation, grammar, diction); organization; reasoning; content. Out of these grades a student, sufficiently motivated, can construct his own commentary and seek such specific help as he needs.

Laboratory hour. After themes have been returned a teacher may set the class to work on correction and then tour the room, stopping to discuss a paper with this or that student, according to a schedule he has worked out from the actual reading. Even in such makeshift conferences a prepared teacher may teach one student more in a few minutes than in hours of time directed to the whole class. Some schools add a "laboratory hour" to the class schedule for students needing special assistance, while those who do not need it are engaged in other activities.

Sampling. The teacher may work out a schedule for each class to guarantee that some of the papers get a careful reading each time while others are only scanned. To be successful such a schedule should be frankly explained to students, but the time at which any given student's paper will get full attention should not be specified. Over a full year perhaps a third of everyone's papers could thus be criticized carefully; in the meantime all students would have the salutary experience of regular writing and motivation to write well. It is only fair to note that, where this system has been tried, students have sometimes objected on the ground that, if they worked hard to write a composition, they deserved at least a reading from the teacher. Many teachers, too, feel uncomfortable about the procedure as an evasion of responsibility. In the long run, neither objection is final, but the situations that produce them may make an alternative procedure preferable. One such alternative is selective analysis in which the teacher reads with attention to only one or two aspects at a time—to organization, for instance, or to argument or diction.

Correcting of mechanical faults by students. A common procedure is to have students exchange papers and correct errors in spelling, punctuation, and the like before the papers go to the teacher at all. Though there is little or no gain in economy of time for the teacher, since he must check the corrections, students themselves profit by being called on to act as "editors" of their fellows' texts.

Class demonstration. This method, too, may serve as a substitute for the complete reading of every paper, and it is useful even when complete reading is possible. For a demonstration, two or three short themes, or sections from several bearing on a particular point of concern, are duplicated and distributed to the class or displayed by an opaque or overhead projector. The papers may be kept anonymous, though in small classes, matters may go better when the author is identified and must defend or explain his performance. If the demonstration is to be useful, the specimens should have enough in common to make comparison possible, and they should represent various ways of solving the assigned problem even more often than they represent various ways of failing to solve it. The class, directed by the teacher, should take an active part in making decisions: first, about what the papers actually say; second, about what is commendable; third, about the serious faults, especially of obscurity, ambiguity, and incompleteness; fourth, about what might be done to make the papers better; finally, about the relative value—all things considered—of the specimens in hand. Such a demonstration combines two important matters: tight focus on a problem of sufficient general importance to warrant attention by the whole class and vigorous criticism from a live and varied audience. Any method of making a writer feel that what he has written and how he has written it are worth serious attention is a good method. And if the teacher directs the criticism of the theme as carefully as he would that of a work of literature, he can make the reaching of some agreement about the text a matter of learning and thus show the student how much a writer must have his wits about him when he sits down to write.

However he goes about it, the teacher is concerned to improve students' style, but he can only help students to find a style or to improve their style by helping them to define their own attitudes. This fact in large measure explains the long history of the preeminence of rhetoric in all western education. It explains why English continues to be thought of as the center of humanistic education. Teachers can hound students to spell correctly, punctuate according to the rules, write complete sentences, avoid dangling modifiers and faulty parallelism—and all these things they must do. But they must make clear that correctness, important as it is in one sense, does not touch the heart of the matter. Style is a matter of control, and until a student recognizes that his character as well as his reputation is involved when he writes he will not take style seriously.

In the end, it is the matter of character that most justifies emphasis on composition in its advanced forms. Pretentiousness and carelessness, for example, are vastly more important targets for criticism than such expressions as "the reason is because," "I contacted him," "the problem is centered around," "different than," and "the data is." Or let us say that whatever importance such expressions have derives not so much from their abrogating a rule as from their exhibiting another fault, lack of respect for a defensible decorum of language, the same lack of respect as is shown by the use of jargon, by wordiness, by clumsy syntax. What students need most is an awareness of the tremendous power of good writing, writing composed of words carefully chosen to control meaning and communicate it precisely.

Of the three conventional divisions of rhetorical theory—invention, style, organization—two have already been discussed. Invention has to do with finding things to say and is, therefore, directly appropriate to the making and scrutiny of assignments. Style, though in classical rhetoric it included elaborate catalogues of figures of speech, is in our time largely a matter of finding language appropriate to the subject, the audience, and the character of the writer. The third division, organization, is that part of rhetoric at which student and teacher can work with greatest likelihood of easy agreement. Simply put, organization is the ordering of parts to meet the demands of clarity. As a matter of fact, whenever the teacher asks critical questions about the structure of a literary work he is also dealing directly with organization. To study the order of argument in a sonnet or the order of elements in a description or the order of episodes in a plot is to study arrangement. But for the purposes of teaching composition, essays of various kinds—formal and informal expositions, arguments and statements of opinion—are the most useful. Such essays serve as well to supply propositions for theme assignments, matter for comparison of styles and for the testing of argumentative patterns. Preeminently, however, they are useful as demonstrations in the anatomy of prose. In most cases, once the sense of the essay is clear, the first question that should be put about it is, "How is this essay organized; what is the order of its parts?" To dissociate the organization from its general sense is no simple matter, and it is clear from the reaction of most college freshmen that they have had little or no experience in examining structure as a thing in itself. Since students learn much from imitation, it is from such analytical study of structure they are likely to learn most for their own compositional purposes, and even in the early high school years it should therefore be a routine part of instruction.

The answers to the primary question stated above should become familiar to every student: here the writer defines, here he restates, summarizes, shows cause and effect, presents successive steps in a process, follows the chronology of events or distorts the actual chronology, makes a comparison, adduces an example or an illustration, proposes an analogy, makes a concession or a qualification, announces an intention or an accomplishment, provides a transition. Out of this habit of naming the order of parts, a student will soon develop skill in detecting what kinds of order appear: logical or psychological (associative), classificatory, cumulative or analytical, inductive or deductive, and the like. The point of such naming goes beyond the acquisition of a vocabulary, useful for the teacher's communication with a student about his theme. This practice is most important because it helps the young writer to understand that more is necessary than invention and style. The order in professional writing, even in that which seems most informal, is seldom the result of a flash of inspiration; after the inspiration, if not with it, must come a conscious exercise of control.

In the study of order, logic presents particular difficulty. It is a subtle science at its best, and efforts to make it part of formal instruction often leave both teacher and student dissatisfied if not bewildered. The English teacher who knows any logical system well enough to teach it properly is rare, and even if he knows it well enough he may reasonably wonder if the weeks such teaching takes achieve as much as time spent otherwise. Other teachers, no less than he, must face this problem, for history, mathematics, and the sciences all depend for their authority on the exercise of a logical faculty.

It is reasonable, then, for the English teacher to commit himself only to those logical problems most often encountered in discursive writing: the broad differences between inductive and deductive argument, the sense in which all rhetorical arguments are contingent, the usefulness but final invalidity of arguments by analogy, and—most common of all —the slipperiness of enthymeme or argument in which an essential part is omitted because it is assumed rather than stated. Again, professional expository essays and students' papers will suffice as texts if the teacher knows clearly the few matters of logic he wants to teach, for most human discourse consists of propositions so arranged as to be subject to rules of logic. And many literary works will take on new life for students if they recognize that in them, too, logic is at work, that they contain propositions no less deserving challenge than those in a formal argument. "If winter comes, can spring be far behind?" will tax no head very far, but it contains a logical proposition as surely as does "If France insists on making a hydrogen bomb, the United States should raise the tariff on French imports." "Shall I compare thee to a summer's day?" begins a sonnet, but it raises at the same time what might be called the "logic" of comparisons, just as Pope's "True ease in writing comes from art, not chance, / As those move easiest who have learned to dance" raises that of analogy. Wherever the mind is at work, logic and accidental or deliberate violations of it mark its progress. As with other kinds of order, students need to know, quite consciously, that such is the case.

One mark of a professional writer is his assumption that whatever he writes may have to be revised or completely rewritten and his consequent persistence in pushing through the hard work that transforms his first version into something clear enough, strong enough, and handsome enough to make its way alone in the world. Writing is full of chances for discovery; it lets the writer live in the character of the speaker whose voice he assumes; like dreaming, it may pleasantly intoxicate. But most rewriting, though it has rewards, is painful. The profit from it must, then, be made commensurately great, not a routine "correction" but a thorough-going revision that in improving the original improves the writer himself. If they can possibly manage it, English teachers should try to show each student at least once a term what is involved in being a serious writer, show him how superficial were whatever tinkering and revising he may have done before submitting his essay in comparison with the substantial revisions a good, stern editor would suggest. The teacher must not kill whatever it is that makes a student willing to try his hand but owes it to him also to show him that when authors talk of the "lonely misery" of writing, they are not talking about first drafts. The pedagogical truth about instruction in writing lies somewhere between twentieth-century emphasis on the joy of learning and the classical emphasis on disciplined thought and precise expression. On that middle ground the teacher of composition takes his stand.

Appendix A.
Examples of Criticism

In the section of this report entitled "The Critical Process," the claim is made that there are certain fundamental questions about a piece of literature, answers to which are necessary for a thorough understanding of the work. These questions the teacher must face as he prepares for class; he must then help his students to answer them as they study the work with him. On page 58 appears a list of these questions, and in the discussion of them which follows that page, a number of brief illustrations are given.

To demonstrate that these questions are useful in coming to grips with a literary work as a whole, the Commission presents three examples of analysis. Two of these, discussing a short essay by E. B. White, were written independently by teachers in the Commission's Summer Institutes of 1962. The third, by Professor Harry Levin, is his critical introduction to *The Scarlet Letter.*

A reprint of White's essay is followed by the two critiques by teachers; a reprint of Levin's introduction is followed by an analysis showing how a professional critic, albeit quite unconsciously—Levin could not have been aware of the list—has answered these "fundamental questions" in the course of elucidating the structure, the meaning, and the value of a classic novel.

EDUCATION*

I have an increasing admiration for the teacher in the country school where we have a third-grade scholar in attendance. She not only undertakes to instruct her charges in all the subjects of the first three grades, but she manages to function quietly and effectively as a guardian of their health, their clothes, their habits, their mothers, and their snowball engagements. She has been doing this sort of Augean task for twenty years, and is both kind and wise. She cooks for the children on the stove that heats the room, and she can cool their passions or warm their soup with equal competence. She conceives their costumes, cleans up their messes, and shares their confidences. My boy already regards his teacher as his great friend, and I think tells her a great deal more than he tells us.

The shift from city school to country school was something we worried about quietly all last summer. I have always rather favored public school over private school, if only because in public school you meet a greater variety of children. This bias of mine, I suspect, is partly an attempt to justify my own past (I never knew anything but public schools) and partly an involuntary defense against getting kicked in the shins by a young ceramist on his way to the kiln. My wife was unacquainted with public schools, never having been exposed (in her early life) to anything more public than the washroom of Miss Winsor's. Regardless of our backgrounds, we both knew that the change in schools was something that concerned not us but the scholar himself. We hoped it would work out all right. In New York our son went to a medium-priced private institution with semi-progressive ideas of education, and modern plumbing. He learned fast, kept well, and we were satisfied. It was an electric, colorful, regimented existence with moments of pleasurable pause and giddy incident. The day the Christmas angel fainted and had to be carried out by one of the Wise Men was educational in the highest sense of the term. Our scholar gave imitations of it around the house for weeks afterward, and I doubt if it ever goes completely out of his mind.

His days were rich in formal experience. Wearing overalls and an old sweater (the accepted uniform of the private seminary), he sallied forth at morn accompanied by a nurse or a parent and walked (or was pulled) two blocks to a corner where the school bus made a flag stop. This flashy vehicle was as punctual as death: seeing us waiting at the cold curb, it would sweep to a halt, open its mouth, suck the boy in, and spring away with an angry growl. It was a good deal like a train picking up a bag of mail. At school the scholar was worked on for six or seven hours by half a dozen teachers and a nurse, and was revived on orange juice in mid-morning. In a cinder court he played games supervised by an athletic instructor, and in a cafeteria he ate lunch worked out by a dietitian. He soon learned to read with gratifying facility and discernment and to make Indian weapons of a semi-deadly nature. Whenever one of his classmates fell low of a fever the news was put on the wires and there were breathless phone calls to physicians, discussing periods of incubation and allied magic.

In the country all one can say is that the situation is different, and somehow more casual. Dressed in corduroys, sweatshirt, and short rubber boots, and carrying a tin dinner-pail, our scholar departs at crack of dawn for the village school, two and a half miles down the road, next to the cemetery. When the road is open and the car will start, he makes the journey by motor, courtesy of his old man. When the snow is deep or the motor is dead or both, he makes it on the hoof. In the afternoons he walks or hitches all or part of the way home in fair weather, gets transported in foul. The schoolhouse is a two-room frame building, bungalow type, shingles stained a burnt brown with weather-resistant stain. It has a chemical toilet in the basement and two teachers above stairs. One takes the first three grades, the other the fourth, fifth, and sixth. They have little or no time for individual instruction, and no time at all for the esoteric. They teach what they know themselves, just as fast and as hard as they can manage. The pupils sit still at their desks in class, and do their milling around outdoors during recess.

There is no supervised play. They play cops and robbers (only they call it "Jail") and throw things at one another—snowballs in winter, rose hips in fall. It seems to satisfy them. They also construct darts, pinwheels, and "pick-up sticks" (jackstraws), and the school itself does a brisk trade in penny candy, which is for sale right in the classroom and which contains "surprises." The most highly prized surprise is a fake cigarette, made of cardboard, fiendishly lifelike.

The memory of how apprehensive we were at the beginning is still strong. The boy was nervous about the change too.

The tension, on that first fair morning in September when we drove him to school, almost blew the windows out of the sedan. And when later we picked him up on the road, wandering along with his little blue lunch-pail, and got his laconic report "All right" in answer to our inquiry about how the day had gone, our relief was vast. Now, after almost a year of it, the only difference we can discover in the two school experiences is that in the country he sleeps better at night—and *that* probably is more the air than the education. When grilled on the subject of school-in-country *vs.* school-in-city, he replied that the chief difference is that the day seems to go so much quicker in the country. "Just like lightning," he reported.

In the following "essays in criticism" the teachers aimed at two goals: to express the observations, insights, and discoveries about White's piece they had made and would hope to help their classes make, and to illustrate the principles of the teacher as critic which they had discussed together and about which they had reached a consensus. They wrote independently, and the differences in style and emphasis in the two critiques argue that a consensus on method does not impair individuality. The similarities in their observations and judgments, however, suggest that answers to the "fundamental questions"—the procedures indicated in "The Critical Process"—provide a satisfactory basis for teaching as well as for the private practice of criticism.

Marginal glosses for the first critique refer to some of the questions listed on page 58. Since the scope of the second critique is less extensive, it does not seem to need glosses.

Critique I

"The Art of the Natural" (Formal Questions)

The reader of E. B. White's six paragraphs called "Education" (in *One Man's Meat*, under the notation, "March 1939") is perhaps not immediately moved to turn for a second look. The essay, in a casual style with its art well concealed, has ended firmly and satisfyingly. The contrast between a village school (with two rooms and two teachers) and a "semi-progressive" "private seminary" in New York (with a half dozen teachers, a nurse, a dietitian, and an athletic instructor) is complete, and the village school has won. Or has it? A doubt begins to paw for attention. The comparison of the two schools that his son attended has led to White's rather unexpected denial that there is, in the end, a definable difference: "... the only difference that we can discover in the two school experiences is that in the country he sleeps better at night—and *that*

What does it mean? (A problem to be considered)

probably is more the air than the education." Yet the boy himself declares at the end of the essay that in the country school the day goes by much faster: " 'Just like lightning,' he reported." Is the difference then a difference without a distinction? Or is our first impression correct, that the distinction is important? How do we know so clearly, in spite of White's denial, that the change of schools was momentous though perhaps not critical?

What kind is it?

As we re-read and think back over the essay we see that one clue to an answer may lie in the fact that the essay is not an essay exactly. It is a mixture of discourses—part essay, part story, in all something like a letter in its casual, but not at all untidy or accidental, organization. From one perspective, the essay is composed of at least three kinds of discourse that correspond to three shifts in the writer's viewpoint. The first viewpoint is that of the personal "letter-writer" (first-person singular) who begins, "I have an increasing admiration for the teacher in the country school...." This "I" is the father of the boy ("My boy") and he favors ("This bias of mine...") the public school, as the boy will do also at the end. This viewpoint gives way to a second, that of a husband who with his wife, or on her behalf (first-person plural) speaks well of the "electric, colorful, regimented existence" that "our scholar" led in the private school ("...and we were satisfied"). The third mode, viewpoint, or kind of discourse is more judicial and ironic (third-person singular). It is this one that says, "In the country all one can say is that the situation is different and somewhat more casual." The "scholar" also is referred to in three ways corresponding to the three viewpoints: as "My boy," "our scholar," and finally and simply as "the boy," who in the final sentence renders the last of the several verdicts—" 'Just like lightning,' he reported."

What are its parts? (Point of view)

How are these parts related? (Sequences)

The sequence of parts corresponds to this succession of viewpoints. In the first paragraph the father praises the village school teacher whom the boy regards as "his great friend." The next paragraph is retrospective as

114

the husband recalls how "we worried" about the shift of "our scholar" from the private to the public school. There follow three paragraphs describing the schools and contrasting them point for point. The more judicious and analytical tone of this central section is that of the relatively detached "third-person," who retains the father's "bias" but also shows the husband's respect for the dissimilar feelings of his wife, who was "unacquainted" with public and country schools. In these three paragraphs the reader senses most keenly the interplay of the several viewpoints now combined. The relatively cool surface of the orderly comparison tenses against the warmth of underlying feelings. The final paragraph, narrating climactically the events of the boy's first venture into the country school, returns to the husband's viewpoint ("... how apprehensive we were at the beginning ..."), only to shift suddenly though unobtrusively to the voice of "the boy," speaking in direct quotation and having the last word in the argument and the story: "'Just like lightning,' he reported."

What we can now discern in our pursuit of convergent meanings is that this "essay" is an argument worked through an analytical contrast of two schools that embody different approaches to education and that the essay is also, structurally, a narrative that ends in climactic scene or anecdote. The essay has the inner form of a story with a surprisingly large cast of characters (or of a few characters playing several roles) who reflect developing stages of the argument and express different shades and mixtures of feeling about the action of the story. The characters (to treat the essay "viewpoints" in terms now of narrative) are a father with his "bias" toward the public school ("... partly an attempt to justify my own past ..."), a husband sharing his wife's hopes and apprehensions; a third more detached and anonymous judge and ironist—perhaps not a "character" but that elusive figure, "the author"; the wife—least visible of the cast—whose favorable disposition to the "private seminary" is part of the

(Other constituents?)

tension of attitudes in the third-person—"author's" viewpoint; and final-

What is the sum of the parts?

ly the boy, with his three roles: son of the father, son of the wife and the husband, and at last, triumphantly, "the boy" himself. Having gained a measure of independence as a character and as a person, he speaks the last words with authority.

What unifies the argument and the story and reconciles the three viewpoints (father, husband, judicial ironist) is the boy's verdict, spoken in his own "laconic" style, a synthesis of the dialectic. So, we see that the casual style concealed a great deal of art, and our first impression was an oversimplification. The argument and story did not simply end in the vindication of the good old-fashioned school at the expense of the semi-progressive one, in a victory (if a polite one) of the husband over his wife, and in a father's justification of his own past by identifying himself with his son. That interpretation is inadequate partly because such an argument is trite, such a victory dubious, and such self-justification facile. Trite, dubious and facile the essay is not. The multiplication of charac-ters, the mixing of kinds of discourse, the rendering of several "verdicts,"

(Testing multiple hypotheses)

all suggest that no simple or "binary" interpretation will prove adequate. In other words, the outcome of the argument and the story is not a cheap victory but a resonance.

The point, we begin to see, is not what is bad about the city school. It is not bad. The father confesses his bias, recognizes his temptation to jus-tify himself, and preserves his good humor. The point of the essay lies in what is good about the school in the country. What is good about it is its

(Reinterpreta-tion)

naturalness; in the words of the judicial ironist, "it is somehow more casual." What is good is that the school is "two and a half miles down the road, next to the cemetery," that the boy leaves for school at "crack of dawn" and gets there "courtesy of his old man" or "on the hoof." What is good is that the schoolhouse is a "bungalow type," "stained a burnt brown," and that in it the two teachers go about their proper business without fuss or pretension, though with professional spirit: "They teach what they know themselves, just as fast and as hard as they can." It is natural for the pupils to "do their milling around outdoors," and to "throw things at one another—snowballs in winter, rose hips in fall." The seasons, rather than an athletics instructor, regulate the games. The school itself salutes the natural appetites of the pupils by doing "a brisk trade in penny candy" with "surprises" in it. It is reassuring that after the boy's first day in the two-room school, his parents pick him up, "on the road, wandering along with his little blue lunch-pail," and get his "laconic report 'All right,' " when they ask how the first day went. This

What does it mean? naturalness—personal and complex—is hard to present except concretely. Because the natural is concrete, personal and complex, the style of the school and of the boy's life is "casual." Such a style, White implies, is something you live in, rather than talk about. Except perhaps in a crisis.

The move from city to country was something of a crisis, and White talks about it from these several viewpoints, through argument and narrative, that permit him to suggest a variety of generalizations without their getting off into abstractions where the concrete and personal, casual and natural, begin to disappear into general systems.

During the larger crisis of the years in which this piece and the others in *One Man's Meat* were written, White wrote another essay a year or so

(Comparison with another work) later, on "Freedom," in which he went about as far as he could go (which is pretty far) toward setting down an explicit testament of political and more than political faith in the time of aggressive fascism and erupting war. The essay on freedom may help us to see why *both* schools described in "Education" are accepted, though one is preferred, why it was significant that the boy slept well in the country and his time in school passed quickly, and why it was well to say so in this casual and complicated way.

The part of the essay on freedom that clarifies these issues concerns a distinction White sees between two kinds, or rather "parts" of freedom as he has experienced it. The first part is "instinctive," he says, "a sense of living somewhat freely in a natural world." It is "a pact which a man has with himself" (the reader will remember the boy "hoofing" the two and a half miles to school) "to stand self-reliant, taking advantage of his haphazard connection with a planet, riding his luck, and following his bent with the tenacity of a hound." This part of freedom man "experiences as an animal dweller on a planet." This freedom the boy has begun to find in the country. "To be free, in a planetary sense, is to feel that you belong to the earth," somewhat as the school belongs to the road beside the cemetery, a school that "somehow" cooperates with the air itself to give the boy better sleep at night. It is "somehow more casual."

The second kind or part of freedom that man experiences is "the practical liberties he enjoys as a privileged member of human society." "To be free, in a social sense, is to feel at home in a democratic framework." This freedom the boy experienced also in the semi-progressive school, where if existence was "formal" (emphasizing the "framework") it was also "rich," "colorful," "electric," with "moments of pleasurable pause and giddy incident." Nor is the village school itself unregimented ("The pupils sit still at their desks in class . . ."). "Somehow more casual" does not mean unstructured. The private school, says White, was a good and satisfactory school, though we may suspect him of some casual joshing with his wife (as with his readers) about the tendency of educational techniques and specialists to be taken too solemnly and theoretically.

What the country school has, then, is both kinds of freedom, especially the first "instinctive," "planetary," "haphazard" kind, which interfered not at all with the teachers' teaching expertly. All this is why time passes quickly. The school has preserved its alliance with the forces of nature. As one of the simplest and most mysterious energies or forms of nature, felt deeply in conscious and unconscious ways, time itself is casual

(Answer to the original question)

118

and free: "Just like lightning."

White's essay on education is visible now not as a tractate stubbornly defending an old-fashioned and disappearing institution against the claims of new fangled and possibly totalitarian progressivism. No such polarity is established. It is an essay in praise of freedom not of an abstract kind, of freedom lived, and lived in society. How is it lived? It is lived, says White, in a casual style, an exact style, a complex and natural style, which demands all the art one can bring to it.

Is it any good?

Critique II

"Humane Education" (Rhetorical Questions)

Of the four people in this piece (the teacher, the son, the mother, and the father) only the last, the "speaker," is an interesting character. In fact, the speaker of this piece is not only the central character, so to speak, he is almost the subject. If we think about what we liked best about the piece, we are very likely to conclude it is the speaker. He is an attractive and admirable human being, we think. We like his honesty in suggesting that his preference for public school is in fact a prejudice, in admitting that his son "learned fast and kept well" in the private school, and in concluding that he sees no essential difference between the public school and the private school. We like his self-knowledge, that enabled him to see a possible source for his prejudice and to describe the two schools in such a way as to reveal his own attitudes without being explicit about them. We even like him for the suggestion of his resentment of his wife's sheltered rearing: the washroom at Miss Winsor's School was no more public than the classroom—why does he mention the washroom at all? It was, in fact, less public than the classroom; and she had been exposed therefore to something more public than the washroom. Why washroom? We'll never know; but we do feel behind the joke a kind of ten-

sion we think we recognize. We are glad for the recognition because the
tension seems to enrich, or make more valuable, the parents' love for
their son: "We knew that the change in schools was something that concerned not us but the scholar himself. We hoped it would work out all
right." And later "The memory of how apprehensive we were at the beginning is still strong" (presumably, the speaker was not so apprehensive as his wife—he shared her apprehension). His love for his wife and
his son (as well as for good manners, for decency, and truth) accounts
for the way he almost suppresses his pleasure in having been right all
along about public schools: that "the day seems to go so much quicker
in the country" is proof enough from the point of view of the father. But
there was not only his love for his boy (and his wife), but his admiration
for the teacher, to keep him from being self-centered. We think we
understand something about him from his admiration of the teacher (he
once loved *his* teacher); but we feel confident in making conclusions
about what he likes and dislikes. The dislike of "getting kicked in the
shins by a young ceramist on his way to the kiln" is balanced by the ap-
proval implied in "The pupils [in the country school] sit still at their
desks in class, and do their milling around outdoors during recess." He
likes things the way they used to be. He likes the old discipline; he mistrusts (or resents—or is afraid of?) the new freedom. Or is it only "the
esoteric" (pottery in first grade) that he mistrusts? For he clearly dislikes the regimentation of the private school. Part of his feeling about the
"half dozen teachers and a nurse" and the "dietitian" and the "athletic
instructor" seems to be directed at the pretentiousness of the school. The
country school, he tells us, "has a chemical toilet in the basement and
two teachers above stairs," and the language, the rhetorical figure linking
unlike things, takes care of the private school's pretensions. But something more serious worries him about the private school: for all its care
about the health, and presumably about the mind and psyche of the stu-

dents, it pretty clearly seems to the father to be impersonal—"formal," "regimented." Even the school bus is monstrous, or non-human—like a machine, or a beast. In the country, though there is no monkey-business, all the discipline and routine are human—established and maintained by a very clearly non-specialist *human* being, who can "cool passions and warm soup with equal competence." In short we admire him for the things he loves and hates and for the intensity with which he does so.

This intensity we feel in the way he says things. We can't separate his feeling from his imagination, which furnishes him with his expression. Wit is a kind of happy union of imagination and passion, and the speaker's wit is, of course, one of the things that attracts us so strongly: "Guardian of . . . their mothers and their snowball engagements"; "cleans up their messes and shares their confidences"; "kicked in the shins by a young ceramist on his way to the kiln"; "more public than the washroom of Miss Winsor's"; "he sallied forth at morn" (compare "departs at crack of dawn"); "punctual as death" (compare "village school, two and a half miles down the road, next to the cemetery"). His love for the plain country virtues comes out in "carrying a tin dinner-pail" and his tenderness for his young son in "his little blue lunch-pail." In fact, of course, we are attracted to the speaker by our admiration for his art—for whatever it is in his character that makes him see things as he does and for whatever it is in his gift and practical skill that enables him to express his vision. It may be that we are attracted by the sanity (the health) he seems to stand for. The "regimented existence" of the private school was also "electric," and the fainting angel and the "breathless phone calls to physicians, discussion periods of incubation and allied magic" hint at his disquiet at something a little too tense, or almost neurotic. His pleasure in the "fake cigarette, made of cardboard, fiendishly lifelike" seems to be another way of asserting his confidence in the health of natural "exposure" to life.

What shall we call the occasion of this piece? "Now, after almost a year" of the public, country school the parents are convinced that their son is as well off as he was in the private, city school. Or, now the father is convinced that he was right in the argument with his wife about public and private schools. Or, in reviewing the change and trying to account for the success of the country school, he decided to write in praise of the teacher, in which case she can be said to be the occasion.

And to whom is the speaker speaking? What do we know about his assumptions about the audience? The informality of the language implies friendliness—equality of a sort. He assumes the audience to consist of people who can be made interested in a story about himself, his family, and two schools—an audience that might enjoy reading diaries. The tone is that of a letter, and implies that sort of limited audience of men with similar tastes implied by most works in the long history of the epistle. They are city people, sophisticated about such things as semi-progressive education, including "kilns." The reference to Miss Winsor's implies an even more "in" group—those who know something about the reputation of The Winsor School in Boston—though those who do not recognize the allusion can be expected to get the force of the passage by assuming that Miss Winsor's is a "private seminary." But more important than sophistication is the urbanity of the audience, that consensus about manners, good taste, *and* decently clothed principles that Horace, an earlier letter-writer, assumed in his audience. Our speaker's audience includes, we feel sure, his wife and the teachers at the private school—or at least *we* know that he thought of them as he tried to say *politely* what he wanted to say.

Now historically, or biographically, what can we know about the piece that is relevant to our understanding of it? If we read other pieces by E. B. White, we will probably be impressed by the integrity of the "speaker"—the man speaking throughout his works is all of a piece. From his early *New Yorker* pieces, collected in a volume called *Quo Vadimus,* to his latest pieces, in *The Points of My Compass,* though we may trace some changes consistent with the change from youth to age and from beginning writer to master, we see how the character and the view of life of the speaker in "Education" is revealed over and over again. White's speaker is always a Horatian satirist, concerned with men and women and things and thoughts and institutions in the here and now; he is always able to talk about himself in such a way as to make the subject not himself but his world, i.e., the world of his audience, in the way Montaigne did. With very little trouble we could show how his early satires on radio press-agentry, on modern advertisements, on successful ministers, and phony stunts done in the name of science are of a piece with the political essays from the late thirties through the essays on the U.N., and with the late pieces on the suspension of Pullman service on the trains between New York and his summer home. The other works of White will also illuminate the speaker in this essay in other ways: we learn that it is Maine that he's moved to and that his wife is a writer and editor. We learn more about his son, and his relations with his son. Finally, beyond his own works, we can learn from pieces written *about* E. B. White some facts that may enrich our understanding of the speaker in his essays—not much, perhaps, but something—even as a photograph of E. B. White is not irrelevant.

White's own life in New York City and his well-described love of the city have some bearing on his romantic view of life in the country, just as Horace's great love of Rome bears on the *Beatus ille* ode. The professional life he shared with his wife on the staff of the *New Yorker* bears on our understanding of his feelings about their son—though it might be hard to say exactly how. Finally, his apprenticeship as a writer under Ross, that most demanding of editors, as well as his earlier study under Professor Strunk at Cornell, bears upon our study of White's combination of great power and great simplicity—upon his art of the informal.

As for the historical occasion of the essay, perhaps we needn't say more than that it was published in March, 1939, when White and his audience were preoccupied by the threats of war. Six months before, in September, 1938 (2 months before *Kristallnacht*) White had written a note from his farm, as follows:

"While the old wars rage and new ones hang like hawks above the world, we, the unholy innocents, study the bulb catalogue and order one dozen paper-white Grandi-flora Narcissus (60 cents) to be grown in a bowl of pebbles. To the list which my wife made out I have added one large root of bleeding heart, to remind us of dead Christians and living Jews."

And six months later he was to write a brief account of what he and his family did on "the Sunday when England and France finally lost their patience." In the months between there had been references to the Nazis. In a fairly short space we could show how the immediate "occasion" of the piece we studied may be related to the larger occasions which inform, or add meaning to, the comparison of the private school and the public school.

One other aspect of the historical "occasion" is that the piece was written for "One Man's Meat," a monthly column written by White for *Harper's Magazine.* The title has some bearing on the meaning of—on the way we read—the piece, as does the Foreword to the collection of essays published under the same title in 1942.

Finally, the historical audience was, of course, readers of *Harper's Magazine,* men and women of a certain age and culture in 1941.

Of the "fundamental questions" (see "The Critical Process"), critique II addresses itself explicitly only to those listed under I.B., "Questions of rhetoric." In the course of determining who is the speaker, the audience, and the occasion, it answers, at least by implication, some of the other questions. For instance, "What kind of work is it?" (I.A., 1) has an implied answer in the suggestion that the "speaker" of White's essay is a satirist like Horace and talks about himself as Montaigne did. Again, some of the "Questions about meaning" (I.C., 3, 4) are answered by implication in the description of the character of the speaker, and "Questions about personal response" (II.A., 1) find more than a partial answer at the beginning and ending of the first paragraph of the critique.

In his introduction to *The Scarlet Letter,* Harry Levin was providing a prefatory essay to a school edition of a classic, to help teachers and students understand and enjoy the novel, just as teachers in class aim to help their students achieve the same ends. His critique is presented not with the implication that any good teacher should be able to do in the classroom what Levin does in this introduction, but in the belief, first, that his critique is valuable in itself, and, second, that its method can be applied, with modifications, by teachers willing to educate themselves, as far as possible, in the kinds of knowledge Levin uses. His essay is printed as it appears in the Riverside Edition of *The Scarlet Letter,* with paragraph and line numbers to facilitate use of the analysis that follows.

Introduction*

HARRY LEVIN

I WE SPEAK of a book as a classic when it has gained a place for itself in our culture, and has consequently become a part of our educational experience. But the term conveys further meanings implying precision of style, formality of structure, and, above all, concern for the basic principles that animate 5 and regulate human behavior. Evaluated by these criteria, the list of unquestioned American classics is not a lengthy one. Often, with oblique regard for the alphabet, it is headed by *The Scarlet Letter*. This, among Hawthorne's larger works, has been generally rated as his characteristic best. It was also 10 his first book-length narration—if we follow his own judgment in ignoring *Fanshawe,* an unsuccessful effort which went back to his college days. For some dozen years after graduation, he had retired to his mother's house in Salem, where he

*From *The Scarlet Letter,* by Nathaniel Hawthorne, edited by Harry Levin (Boston: Houghton Mifflin Company, 1960), pages vii-xxi. Reprinted by the kind permission of Harry Levin and Houghton Mifflin Company.

experimented with essayistic sketches and didactic tales, most   15
of them evoking the regional past. A series of penny-a-lining
assignments for Boston publishers, a brief job as measurer at
the port of Boston, a season as a member of the utopian settle-
ment at Brook Farm had not tempered that sense of isolation
which underlay his need to communicate. Then his happy   20
marriage and his paradisiac sojourn at Concord had released
those flights of fantasy which reached their haven in *Mosses
from an Old Manse*. But, since such writing was too delicate
to support a growing family, his influential friends secured
him part-time employment as Surveyor of the Revenue in the   25
United States Custom-House at Salem.

II   Wedlock had made him belatedly sympathetic toward
women and the relation between the sexes. Office-holding
made him somewhat ironic about himself and his fellow
office-holders and even the society they served. Given the
austerity of his background plus the reticence of his tempera-   5
ment, both of these responsibilities had been steps to a hard-
won maturity in his mid-forties, for Hawthorne as a man and
as a writer. He admired the intellectuals of Concord and
Cambridge, but he had seen enough of them to realize that
his own mind would never march with any school of thought.   10
After association with Bronson Alcott and Transcendentalism

at its most impractical, he had welcomed "a change of diet."
Yet he felt he must account to readers for his three-and-a-half
years in an ineffectual bureaucracy, as well as for the cir-
cumstances that led to the termination of his appointment. 15
His "autobiographical impulse," which came to the surface
whenever he introduced a new work, joined forces with his
homing instinct, which tended to focus his imagination on
houses of varying kinds. Hence he gave his *Scarlet Letter* a
local habitation by way of his introduction, "The Custom- 20
House." Now that the Whigs had come back into office and
Hawthorne — a staunch, if not an ardent, Democrat — was
out of it, he could resume his true calling, the life of letters.
But first he settled his score with politics, said farewell to his
native town, and reverted to the colonial period, by gathering 25
his latest impressions into a "sketch of official life."

III   That introductory sketch, which is one-fifth as long as the
actual story, seems to have caused more immediate discussion
than what it heralded. It may well have helped to create the
unexpected demand for second and third editions within a few
months. To the second edition Hawthorne added a preface, 5
disclaiming partisan or personal malice, and refusing to delete
or alter a single touch. It would not have become him to wax
indignant over the Spoils System, from which he would benefit

in his turn; instead, with cool amusement and obvious relief, he had set down a few reminiscences of his erstwhile col- 10 leagues. More serious is the objection some critics have leveled at "The Custom-House": that it offers an unsuitable preamble to *The Scarlet Letter* itself. There is indeed a contrast; but it has clearly been calculated; for Hawthorne's art is based on antithesis. It is as if, before conducting us into a realm of 15 shadows, he wished to exhibit worldly substance at its most substantial. Yet the commercial routine of customs inspection harbors internal contrasts of its own. The names of Salem merchants, as entered in ledgers along with their respective imports and tariffs, are balanced against the shades of ancestral 20 Hawthornes, witch-hanging Puritans who would frown upon their scion's weakness for writing story-books. The declining seaport is presented as the ghost of its bustling former self. A passing glance at the Gold Rush reminds us that, by 1849, the pursuit of material wealth had worked its way from New 25 England to California.

IV   But Hawthorne cannot give us more than "a faint representation of a mode of life not heretofore described." Contemplating the page that reality has spread out directly before him, he regrets his inability to probe its commonplaces for deeper significance. "A better book than I shall ever write," he sighs, 5 "was there"—there, in that sphere of concrete observation which others were developing into the modern novel. He never thought of himself as a novelist; he was habitually "a romance-writer." The romance, as he defined it repeatedly, takes place in a twilit half-world "where the Actual and the Imaginary may meet." Hawthorne contrasts his busy days at the custom-house with his dreamy evenings at home in the parlor, where his imaginative faculties reawaken amid the flicker of moonlight and firelight. The evolving shapes, though they seem strange and remote, are the familiar spirits that haunt his fiction: snow-images, soap-bubbles, mirror-reflections. But though he proceeds—through his domestic transition—from the contemporary and realistic to the legendary and symbolic, the shift of direction is not a means of escape. Rather, the quasi-historical setting allows him to question certain moralistic assumptions with a freedom and a candor which he could not have applied to a nineteenth-century subject. It is not the least of the book's achievements that, in the very epoch of genteel femininity, when America outdid Victorian England in the strictness of its taboos, Hawthorne's treatment of a triangle was hardly less of a challenge than D. H. Lawrence's.

V   As a customs officer, Hawthorne could cite such poetic forerunners as Chaucer and Burns, and could set an American

precedent for the later Melville and Edwin Arlington Robin-
son. Moreover, as a keeper of records, he could shift to the
story-teller's ground by employing a conventional device of   5
romantic fiction; he could imagine that he had chanced upon
his material in an ancient manuscript, which he described in
meticulous detail, together with its faded and tattered yet
gorgeous relic, the letter. This lent an air of authenticity to
the tale, while enabling the narrator to assume a tone of edi-   10
torial aloofness. It had the more potent effect of fixing attention upon the searing initial, promising mystery and inviting
speculation from the very outset. Hawthorne's plan for the
volume had been to include a number of shorter pieces; he
mentions two of his neighborhood rambles, "Main Street" and   15
"A Rill from the Town Pump." Many of his earlier stories
had touched upon themes that *The Scarlet Letter* would spell
out: notably "The Maypole of Merry Mount," where bright
color and its studied avoidance emphasized the antagonism
between Cavalier and Puritan views of sex. Frequently he used   20
costume for characterization, as in "Lady Eleanore's Mantle,"
where a sumptuous garment symbolizes the pride of its owner
and carries within it the germs of catastrophe. He was interested in characters who were not only isolated but marked by
all too literal stigmata, such as the heroine of "The Birthmark,"   25

whose imperfection cannot be eradicated because it betokens
Eve's original sin.

VI   In "Endicott and the Red Cross," as the title specifies, the
central object was a different sort of scarlet emblem. But,
among the Salem crowd that has gathered to see the Popish
sign renounced, we are given a memorable glimpse of an
anonymous bystander: 5

> There was likewise a young woman, with no mean share of
> beauty, whose doom it was to wear the letter A on the breast
> of her gown, in the eyes of all the world and her own children.
> And even her own children knew what that initial signified.
> Sporting with her infamy, the lost and desperate creature had   10
> embroidered the fatal token in scarlet cloth, with golden
> thread and the nicest art of needle-work; so that the capital A
> might have been thought to mean Admirable, or anything
> rather than Adulteress.

Hawthorne was fascinated by that stern practice of branding   15
convicted sinners, which he had encountered in his antiquarian
reading. He refined upon it with a paradox, when he permitted
the unnamed hussy to make a decoration out of her insignia of
dishonor. Yet there was no real ambiguity; she was simply
brazening out her shame; even her children knew what A stood   20
for, embellished or otherwise. A jotted hint from a notebook

of 1844, seven years after that fable, records Hawthorne's de-
termination to study more deeply the character of such a
protagonist. Persistently, he realized his intention three years
later, when he undertook *The Scarlet Letter.* He was aware   25
that the abbreviated epithet could not do justice to the full-
scale portrait he was drawing, that moral judgments are not
satisfactorily arrived at by the external application of labels.
The perennial conflict of letter and spirit had been sharpened
for him by the tension between the repressive legalism of   30
Calvinistic tradition, on the one hand, and the Transcendental
urge toward self-expression, on the other. If his starting-point
is condemnation, his objective is to reopen the case. His
heroine's illegitimate child, precocious though she may be,
does not accept or understand the stigma. And, along with   35
her, we are kept wondering: "What does the letter mean,
mother? —and why dost thou wear it? —and why does the
minister keep his hand over his heart?"

VII   The girl has a special affinity with the letter; for, if it is
the mark of her mother's sin, she herself is the outcome and
retribution. She, as her observers recognize, is "the scarlet
letter endowed with life." As such she stands a little outside of
the code that governs the others; like the infant Quaker in   5
Hawthorne's "Gentle Boy," she is cruelly mistreated by the

other children. Not being gentle, she retaliates fiercely, and
acquires a reputation as an imp of evil, perhaps the devil's
offspring. She is more appropriately depicted in the guise of
an elfin sprite, a natural child in the fullest sense of the phrase,   10
happiest when gracefully playing in her element, nature. Innocent enough to have been named Pearl, which signifies
purity as well as great price, nonetheless she is wilder than an
Indian, as wild as a bird or a breeze. She has learned her
capitals in a hornbook; but, though Hawthorne alludes to the   15
New England Primer, she has not mastered its most elementary
lesson, where A stands for the archetypal sinner:

> By *Adam's* fall
> We sinned all.

Her innocence does not exempt her from the inherited evils   20
of the flesh; but it does suggest that, as at the Garden of Eden,
fatal temptations sometimes produce fertile consequences.
Hawthorne was not attempting to subvert the Seventh Com-
mandment or to demonstrate that adulteresses are admirable.
He was concerned to show that fundamental morality is not so   25
much a series of rigorous laws to be enforced by a meddling
community as it is an insight to be attained through continuous
exertion on the part of the individual conscience. Viewed in
that light, it becomes conceivable for the adulteress to outgrow

her discredited role and to grow into so admirable a person as   30
Hester Prynne.

VIII   This kind of growth would be inconceivable if Hawthorne
really were what he has so frequently been taken for, a mere
allegorist. Hester could then do no more than live up to her
label, like Bunyan's personified vices. But that is precisely
where Hawthorne broke through the preconceptions of al-   5
legory to living situations. Though he was fond of pointing
out object lessons or utilizing symbolic counterparts to embody his ideas, those ideas — when charged with feeling —
transcend or transfigure their embodiments. The letter, which
seems naively and narrowly explicit at first, gradually takes   10
on its unique aura of intellectual suggestions and emotional
associations. It is "a forcible type of moral solitude," for worse
or for better: a curse which ostracizes its wearer, and yet —
as the outcast develops morally — a blessing in disguise.
Whereas Lady Eleanore wrapped herself in the mantle of pride,   15
Hester wears the badge of humility. Like "the cross on a
nun's bosom," it has a quality of sacredness; and Indian
weapons seem powerless to transpierce it. More and more, it
proves to be a talisman, though some of the hearsay about it
seems open to doubt — its capacity to burn and glow and to   20
project itself against the sky. At that level, we cannot solve

the enigma, which slips away into the void like Melville's whale. However, we can reconsider the ethical standards whereby Hester has been judged and condemned. Her ambiguous A comes to mean, among other things, angel. Her shameful token is finally visualized, in heraldic terms, as a noble escutcheon upon her tombstone. 25

IX   The book ends, as it begins, in retrospect, so that the characters are framed by the symbolism. In the interim, Hawthorne brings them to life by reinforcing their very resistance to the categories imposed upon them or to the types with which they are compared. Hester may represent, to the grim 5 elders and their self-righteous goodwives "the general symbol at which the preacher and moralist might point, and in which they might vivify and embody their images of woman's frailty and sinful passion." But, from her entrance, she transforms her disgrace into dignity. Her beauty, at odds with her spiritual 10 condition, "made a halo of the misfortune and ignominy in which she was enveloped." Her taste for the beautiful, which has prompted her to embroider the letter, is one of the attributes that set her apart. The dash of red against her gray attire is a constant reminder of the differences between herself 15 and the other colonists, whose somber dress proclaims their cheerless outlook. Moving from the prison to the pillory, she

is forced to stand there in the statuesque pose of the Woman
Taken in Adultery. Yet a Catholic witness, Hawthorne suggests, might—with esthetic justification—have likened her   20
to a more profoundly appealing prototype: a painting of the
Madonna. The Child in her arms is thus, from one point of
view, the confounding evidence of her guilt. From another,
it is the innocent hope of future redemption. Like the letter
by which it is prefigured, it concretely links profane with   25
sacred love; it is the unbreakable bond between the sin and its
expiation.

X   In his European romance, *The Marble Faun,* Hawthorne was
to elaborate his conception of education by sin, of remorse as
the teacher that broadens the sympathies and of suffering as
the discipline that deepens the emotions. Similarly, Hester
finds that her trespass endows her with "a sympathetic knowl-   5
edge of the hidden sin in other hearts." Her ostracism gives
her a vocation. Outlawed by the law-abiding, she is welcome
only where misery prevails. Her good deeds and selfless in-
terventions make her a byword among her fellow sufferers,
and she rehabilitates herself as a Sister of Charity. Meanwhile,   10
the letter has served as "her passport into regions where other
women dared not tread." Liberating her from the conventions
she has violated, it has encouraged her to think more freely

and to form independent notions of right and wrong. Cut off
from the Puritans, she approaches more closely than they to   15
the speculative and skeptical spirit of the age, as expressed by
more enlightened thinkers on the other side of the Atlantic.
Had she been less of a woman and a mother, Hawthorne sur-
mises, she might have become a prophetess like Ann Hutchinson; but her godly neighbors were even harder on their heretics   20
than on their profligates. The alternative was the illicit path
to the forest and to a witches' sabbath. Mistress Hibbins, who
beckons Hester thither, is predestined to be hanged for witch-
craft; yet she insinuates—what Hawthorne illustrates in
"Young Goodman Brown"—that many of the town's re-   25
spectable citizens, with impunity, devote their nights to the
clandestine worship of the devil.

XI   Hawthorne would have us remember that his settlers were
not far from their English origins. They were the near de-
scendants of the Elizabethans; and, though they could not
have inherited the rich fancies of their forbears, something of
the older lore and custom had weathered their harsher climate.   5
Hawthorne's nomenclature catches, at least, the seventeenth-
century atmosphere. Hester is an Anglicized variant of Esther,
the name of the queen who redeemed her people in the Old
Testament. William Prynne was one of the most fanatical of

the English Puritan controversialists. His surname has more   10
pertinently belonged to Hester's husband, who — after making
his appearance incognito—adopts the pseudonym of Roger
Chillingworth. Here cross-reference is less pertinent; for
William Chillingworth was a pioneering exponent of religious
toleration; but Hawthorne seems to be playing upon the re-   15
verberations of "chilling." Two years afterward, in *The
Blithedale Romance,* he would christen his cold-blooded villain
Hollingsworth—an echo paralleled by the chiming names of
the two hesitant heroes, Dimmesdale and Coverdale. As for
Chillingworth, he is the most complete incarnation of a figure   20
which Hawthorne was continually re-examining. This was the
man of intellect whose obsession had deadened his sensibilities,
the scholar-scientist whose experiments dealt ruthlessly with
human lives. Shortly before *The Scarlet Letter,* he had been
adumbrated in "Ethan Brand," but without convincing mo-   25
tivation for his fiendish curiosity. In 1847 Hawthorne had
noted: "A story of the effects of revenge, diabolizing him who
indulges in it."

XII   Our first impression of Chillingworth is a dim one, a face in
a sequence of pictures out of her past which flash through
Hester's mind at the pillory. Within a page or two, she identifies him as the stranger at the edge of the crowd; and he

indicates, by a silent gesture, that the recognition is mutual. 5
For him it is coupled with the shock of discovering how unfaithful she has been in his absence; and she, when he interviews her in prison, refuses to betray the identity of her lover.
Up to this point, the moral superiority is on the side of the
injured party, Chillingworth. He is bookish, elderly, slightly 10
deformed, and entirely incompatible with a young wife, as he
now is ready to admit. Leaving her fate to the auspices of the
letter, he resolves to take the vengeance against his rival into
his own hands. Step by step, he spies out his victim, tortures an
already agonized conscience, and goads it on toward confes- 15
sion; and, in the process, Chillingworth himself is transformed
into a virtual fiend. He is fatalistic about the parts that all
three must enact: "It has all been a dark necessity." Chance
or necessity operates to make Arthur Dimmesdale his fellow
lodger and patient, since the young minister is in waning 20
health, and since the scholar's scientific interests qualify him
as a physician. His equivocal standing, in juxtaposition with
the minister's pious repute, inspires the congregation to believe
that their saintly champion is struggling against a diabolical
agent. The ironic fact, of course, is that Chillingworth has 25
been mortally wronged by Dimmesdale.

XIII   If Chillingworth plays Mephistopheles, he is not trying to beguile Faust into a seduction but to bring out his remorseful afterthoughts. As a doctor, Chillingworth perceives that the source of his patient's malady is not physical. There is "a strange sympathy betwixt soul and body" in Dimmesdale. 5 Ultimately his body reveals the secret his soul has kept. Today we would call his illness psychosomatic, and look upon his colloquies with the leech as sessions with a psychoanalyst. Hawthorne's vocabulary may sound old-fashioned; yet we have scarcely penetrated beyond some of his psychological 10 perceptions, such as his argument for the essential sameness of love and hate—which we might characterize, less elegantly, as the ambivalence of Chillingworth's motives. With Dimmes-dale, the problem is Hawthorne's obsessive theme of secret sin—guilt-consciousness, suppressed and seeking catharsis. 15 He first appears as a model of virtue, praying and exhorting the adulteress to disclose the adulterer, lest her unknown partner "add hypocrisy to sin." That the parson refers to himself is an irony which may pass unnoted, until the scalpel of Chilling-worth's suspicion has laid bare "the interior of a heart." Then, 20 in a "vain show of expiation," Dimmesdale goes through the motions of Hester's exposure. Alone, in the darkness, he as-cends the scaffold. His night-watch is a Hawthornesque medi-tation, not unlike the critical chapter on "Governor Pyncheon"

in *The House of the Seven Gables.* The vision in which it 25
culminates, the letter A etched in red against the heavens, is
either supernatural or subjective—Hawthorne deliberately
equivocates.

XIV   Dimmesdale has undergone penance, but he has not achieved
penitence; he has suffered, he has not been absolved. While
"the outcast woman" is becoming a lay saint, he—"poor,
fallen man"—is being overwhelmed by his unacknowledged
sinfulness. Brilliant, sensitive, esteemed for his learning at 5
Oxford and for his eloquence in the colonies, he is weak where
she is strong. While she has emancipated herself, he is still
entrammeled between his vows and his desires. An encounter
in the woods between "the pastor and his parishioner," as
Hawthorne dryly designates them, threatens to rekindle their 10
latent passion. "What we did," Hester tells Dimmesdale, "had
a consecration of its own." Nature, being heathen, sympathizes
with this renewal; but Pearl remains, significantly, an anti-
pathetic force; and the letter figures as a portent, momentarily
flung into the brook and inexorably cast up again. The adul- 15
terous couple, like Dante's Paolo and Francesca, seem bound
together by the very ties they have broken. They plan an
elopement, a return to the Old World, unaware that the om-
niscient Chillingworth will be making his own plans to ac-

company them. In the meantime, on the day before they are 20
scheduled to sail, the Rev. Mr. Dimmesdale has been accorded
the duty and the honor of preaching an Election Sermon. It is
that moment of triumphant pride which precedes a tragic fall.
Hawthorne leads up to it by tracing Dimmesdale's inner vacil-
lations and conflicting emotions, and by setting the outer stage 25
for a closing scene which releases the pent-up dramatic
suspense.

XV   Hawthorne's art is related to the drama less immediately
than to the pulpit. It is the product of a cultural environment
dominated by the ministry, where a work of fiction—if tol-
erated at all—had to be an *exemplum,* an anecdotal example
illustrating an ethical precept. Typical was Hawthorne's par- 5
able of the black veil put on by a blameless minister in order
to remind his congregation of their undisclosed sins. This is
the opposite of Dimmesdale's concealment, which is exemplified when he compulsively puts his hand over his heart. The
scarlet letter is even more overt than the black veil, and Hester's 10
sentence is intended to convert her into "a living sermon
against sin." But living, as it is practiced by the preacher, does
not square with his sermonizing. His preliminary exhortation
rings hollow; his solitary vigil on the scaffold is an evasion.
Though the Election Sermon, his valediction, stirs its hearers 15

to enthusiastic acclaim, Hester hears only its sorrow-laden undertone. The key modulates from theology to psychology, as it usually does with Hawthorne. At the close of the story, as at the beginning, the chorus of townspeople is seen and heard, placing the situation in social perspective. The holiday, the festive procession, the modest relaxations from "Puritanic gloom" highlight the desperate seriousness of the spokesman for the occasion. His speech is not so much precept as example: he re-ascends the scaffold, bares his breast, and exposes the brand. To be at peace with himself, like Raskolnikov in *Crime and Punishment,* he must publicly confess.

XVI   Unlike Dostoevsky's hero-villain, Dimmesdale has already suffered his punishment, and he willingly yields up his life with his guilty burden. Characteristically, his final action is surrounded with metaphysical uncertainties, leaving readers a choice of interpretations. Thus, if they do not believe in heavenly miracles or in Chillingworth's devilish magic, the emergence of the letter may be rationalized as the result of Dimmesdale's self-laceration. We are even informed of "highly respectable witnesses" who have denied the phenomenon, together with any carnal relationship between the clergyman and the fallen woman, and have interpreted his death in her arms as an exemplary act of Christian humility. But Haw-

thorne pointedly discounts that version. Among the numerous
morals that might be drawn, he stresses chastity or virtuous
conduct less than sincerity and willingness to acknowledge   15
one's faults: "Be true! Show freely to the world, if not your
worst, yet some trait whereby the worst may be inferred!"
Truth is the extenuating virtue to which Hester Prynne has
held fast, despite her transgression. Unfaithful as a wife, she
has not been "false to the symbol on her bosom." Whereas   20
the priest has not only polluted his cloth, but—by playing the
hypocrite—has degraded his virtues into vices, and must
pay heavily for his atonement. Each of the pair is appropriately punished for having broken the sacrament of marriage.
Yet neither is as much to blame as Chillingworth, their victim 25
who has become their accomplice and persecutor. "That old
man's revenge," says Dimmesdale to Hester, "has been blacker
than my sin."

XVII   It has been destructive and self-destroying, whereas their
union—though unhallowed—has been unselfish and has
become creative. This transposition of values is underscored
when Pearl, their visible tie, confuses Chillingworth with the
devil, alias the Black Man. Pearl herself is a "living hiero-   5
glyphic," especially meaningful when bedecked with wild-
flowers. She claims to have come into existence by being

plucked from the rosebush that so symbolically flowers among the weeds at the prison-door. Once she fills in her mother's ornament with prickly burrs; again she outlines a green A 10 upon her own dress in eel-grass. Hawthorne's belief in correspondences between the natural and the spiritual worlds is manifest in all his descriptions of foliage. The doctor picks his mysterious herbs in the graveyard, where they hint unspoken crimes to Dimmesdale. Whatever the idea, it is ren- 15 dered concrete by the image. Conversely, the imagery is emblematic, and always pictures forth—as Hawthorne would say—some concept or other. His descriptive mode is what he elsewhere calls "the moral picturesque." Many of his short stories read like essays, where the moralist discourses about 20 a pictorial illustration. His method of building up a longer narrative is to articulate a chain of such episodes, under captions which are indications of *dramatis personae,* scenic effects, or stage-directions. Each episode dramatically centers on what we might regard as a *tableau vivant,* a group of figures 25 posed in revealing attitudes, summed up in an aphoristic remark by one of them or the implicit comment of some telling detail.

XVIII   Hawthorne's flair for symmetry controls his neat arrangement of chapters, as well as the balanced prose of his sentences.

Apart from its prologue, *The Scarlet Letter* consists of twenty-
four numbered sections, which can be coherently grouped
in twos, threes, fours, and sixes, as readers may notice. The   5
conclusion rounds out a pattern established by the opening
scene, with Hester, then Dimmesdale, in the pillory. Both of
those scenes are public occasions; the latter has had its private
rehearsal at the midpoint, Chapter XII, "The Minister's Vigil."
All three—plus Chapter VII, "The Governor's Hall"—may   10
be considered as ceremonials, bringing the major characters
into the choric presence of the community. These alternate
with more intimate revelations, monologues where consciences
are examined in Hawthornesque solitude, or dialogues where
they confront one another with searching interviews: Hester-   15
Chillingworth, Chillingworth-Dimmesdale, Dimmesdale-Hes-
ter. This trio of principal actors, the parties to the conjugal
involvement, augmented by its elusive consequence, Pearl,
forms a cast succinctly completed by a few minor characters
modeled on historic originals: Richard Bellingham, governor   20
of the colony; John Wilson, senior pastor of Boston; and
Mistress Hibbins, alleged to be a witch. The story moves
along with the rhythm of a detective thriller, quickening as
its network of suspicion tightens and is confirmed. Hester
and Chillingworth recognize each other at the commencement;   25

Chillingworth recognizes Dimmesdale by the middle of the book; and Dimmesdale, Chillingworth midway through the second half.

XIX   The culmination is the recognition-scene where Dimmesdale lays his soul bare to the multitude. As he dies, the purport of the letter becomes a matter of common knowledge. Yet it is more significant for the self-knowledge it has been imparting to those involved with it during the seven probationary years 5 since the beginning, when Pearl was some three months old. Hester, unable to set it aside or to stay away for long, will return to live and die in its service, as we learn from a glancing epilogue. Chillingworth, wilting "like an uprooted weed," will die within a year, bequeathing his considerable fortune to 10 Pearl. Her future, as a young American heiress abroad, may provoke our curiosity; but that is another story, it has been suggested, which might be better left to Henry James. The time-span of *The Scarlet Letter* can be dated by Pearl's infancy: roughly, she is a child in arms for the first four chapters, 15 three years old in Chapters V-VIII, and seven by Chapter XII. These dates can be grounded historically through the allusion to John Winthrop's death—actually March 26, 1649—on the night of the minister's vigil. Twelve more chapters, constituting the second half, culminate about two months after- 20

ward on Election Day. This does not make the tale a historical
novel; in spite of Hawthorne's documentary touches, he is preoccupied with morals, not manners; and his title-page announces "a romance." A romance about Puritanism is bound
to be somewhat contradictory; but here the contradiction is   25
logically resolved through the interplay between puritanical
constraints and romantic impulses, between the rigid observ-
ances of the market-place and the tangled passions of the forest.

XX   More broadly speaking, these alternatives dramatize such
typically American dilemmas as those of introspection against
extroversion, nonconformity against standardization, and skeptical detachment against material progress. What is distinctive
with Hawthorne is his emphasis on the more difficult choice.   5
Ordinarily it seems easier for our authors to depict characters
—for example, John Steinbeck's—rough in outward aspect
but pure in heart. Hawthorne's portraiture is more refined;
yet it catches traits of anguish and terror which, though they
may never be completely eliminated, are blandly masked by   10
the smiling surfaces that a later breed of Americans seems to
prefer. We are told that the Election Sermon projected a
glorious vision of our national destiny; yet the repercussions
we feel are neither hopes nor promises; they are the agonies
of Arthur Dimmesdale. Sin and death are not absent from   15

Utopia, Hawthorne asserts upon his very first page. He did not enjoy his pessimism; he would have preferred to write sunnier books. The few rays of sunlight that shine in *The Scarlet Letter* are associated, through the image of Pearl, with his affection for his own daughter. But his gloomy ancestors maintain the upper hand; and when he speaks of combining recreation with solemnity, his metaphor is an honorific version of the letter itself: "a grotesque and brilliant embroidery to the great robe of state." To have spun an imaginary bit of old cloth into a subtly colored evocation of the Massachusetts Bay Colony, darkly shading toward the wilderness beyond it—the story-teller's skill at making much out of little has seldom been more effectively exercised.

Analysis of Levin's Introduction

To understand the structure of Levin's introduction it is first necessary to answer the second of the questions about form, "What are its parts?" (I.A., 2). This answer can be made in two ways: by showing how the discourse is put together sequentially, unit by unit; and by discovering what different kinds of criticism it contains.

The first answer starts by identifying the largest section of the piece. At line 33 of paragraph VI, where Levin begins to discuss Pearl, he also begins to talk about the novel itself, the contents of the story. After Pearl, he discusses Hester (VIII.1), then Chillingworth (XII), and finally Dimmesdale (XIII.4). This central section, from VI.33 to XVI, constitutes about half of the essay, and may, for convenience, be labeled Part B.

Part A may be called "backgrounds"—a plural word because there are three kinds of this material. After an opening evaluative statement (I.1-10), Levin indicates the historical relationship of the book to Hawthorne's life (I.10-III.3). He then discusses Hawthorne's own introductory sketch, "The Custom-House" (III.13-V.13), and from this point to the end of Part A, he describes the conception and birth, so to speak, of the novel.

Part C, beginning with XVI, contains six topics, all related, but distinct from the historical material of Part A or the explicatory material of Part B. These topics deal with Hawthorne's art and help the reader to understand and evaluate the novel. The topics are as follows: (1) meanings or morals (XVI-XVII.5); (2) mode—symbol, imagery, emblem, descriptive mode in narrative method (XVII.5-end of XVII); (3) structure (XVIII-XIX.19); (4) genre (XIX.19-end of XIX); (5) significance—Hawthorne's view of man's fate (XX.1-XX.24); and (6) evaluation—the excellence of the novel (XX.24 to end). This last topic sums up in different terms the evaluation with which Levin began his piece (I.1-10).

Despite the fact that the essay can be analyzed in this fashion, its organization will appear to the careful reader not as mechanical, but as organic. Answers to the critical questions can be found in all parts of the critique: for example, there is as much about the meaning of the novel in the central exposition, Part B, as in the more explicit answer to that question in Part C. Again, Part B seems at first glance to be merely a series of character sketches, but in fact, Levin says much about plot in this section of his essay.

The second answer to the question about the parts goes beyond any division by topics, like that noted above, to recognize three constituent elements in the essay, three kinds of criticism. One kind requires a knowledge of other literature, of literary history and theory—a remembered stock of knowledge that is one of the distinctions of a good critic. A second kind depends upon knowledge of the author's life, works, and times. The third kind depends on knowledge of the text, and the intelligence and imagination of the critic.

Analysis of the essay according to these three categories of criticism, or qualifications of the critic, is suggested as a valuable exercise. Levin begins his introduction with the first kind: discussions dependent upon his general knowledge of literature. So, in the first eight lines of I he presents a definition, a comparison, and a judgment. IV.22-26 and V.3 contain some general cultural history, a literary comparison, and a bit of literary history. In VI.29-32 and X.16-17, Levin generalizes from his knowledge of intellectual history, and from this same source come his comments on the names Prynne and Chillingworth in XI.9-14. There are a few illuminating references to well-known literary works (VIII.22; XIII.1-3; and XV.25-XVI.1). Finally, XIX.13, 17-18, 21-28; XX.1-8 and 27-28 constitute much of Levin's conclusion and include matters of history, American culture, and literary excellence. All told, this first kind of criticism covers about 52 lines, or about 10 percent of the whole essay.

Of the second kind there is considerably more. This is the criticism that depends upon a knowledge of Hawthorne's life, times, and other writings—material that reading and research will provide any conscientious critic. It is to be found in I.9-III.13; V.13-VI.25; VII.5-6; X.1-4; XI.16-28; XVII.18-21; XX.16-21. These passages together comprise a little more than 20 percent of the whole introduction.

All the rest can be included under the third kind of criticism: that which depends upon a careful reading of the text by a man of good sense, imagination, literary experience, and whatever other faculties, powers, or blessings a good critic needs.

Any reader may, if he wishes, make this kind of analysis more vivid and explicit for himself by the simple process of marking, with pencils of different colors, the various passages identified above as belonging to the first two kinds of criticism. He will find much of the essay still unmarked: most of it, in other words, derives from Levin's imaginative study of the text of *The Scarlet Letter,* apart from, though surely modified by, his knowledge of literature in general and of Hawthorne's biography and environment.

The present analysis has, so far, dealt with two different answers to only one of the questions listed on page 58: "What are its parts?" A careful comparison of the other questions with Levin's introduction, however, will show not only that they are all answered (not, of course, intentionally, and not in the order of their listing), but also that there is little or nothing in the piece that does not fall under one or another of the questions. For those seeking proof of this statement, the following scheme indicates where the answers to most of the questions occur.

I. Questions about the text itself
  A. Questions of form
      1. What is its kind? I.1-6; IV.7-11; VIII.1-9; XV.1-5; XIX.21-28
      2. What are its parts? III.1-2; XVIII-XIX.21
      3. How are the parts related? XVIII-XIX.21
  B. Questions of rhetoric
  (Intrinsic)
      1. Who is speaking?
      2. What is the occasion?
      3. Who is the audience?
          These questions in respect to the narrator are answered in the discussion of "The Custom-House," in IV and especially in V.5-11. In respect to the speakers in the novel, they are answered in most of the central part of the essay (VI.32-XV.26).

  (Extrinsic)
      1. Who is speaking? I.10-III.10; XI.13-28; XX.16-21
      2. What is the occasion? V.13-VI.25
      3. Who is the audience? III.1-13
  C. Questions about meaning
      1. Meaning of words in a particular context? XIII.3-8; XVI.26-XVII.3
      2. What do the diction and grammar tell about its purpose? XVII.5-XVIII.2
      3. What is the paraphrasable content of the work? XVI.13-XVII.3; XIX.24-XX.4
      4. What intention is apparent and how is it made apparent? VI.5-35; XIX.21-28
      5. What part of meaning is sacrificed by paraphrase? Levin notes (XVI.3-13) a deliberate ambiguity, a choice of interpretations, making any single paraphrase impossible.

II. Questions of value

    A. Questions about personal response. Levin, like most critics aiming at objectivity, answers these questions mainly by implication. That his responses were favorable can be inferred from the tone of the introduction as a whole; more specifically, by such passages as IV.19-26; VII.25-31; XIII.9-13.

    B. Questions of excellence. I.1-9; XX.27-28

Appendix B.
Planning Institutes
and Summer Institutes

Participating Universities and Teachers:
Planning Institute, 1961, and the Summer Institutes, 1962

Cornell University, Ithaca, New York . . . .
Duke University, Durham, North Carolina . . . .
Harvard University, Cambridge, Massachusetts . . . .
Indiana University, Bloomington, Indiana . . . .
New York University, New York, New York . . . .
Ohio State University, Columbus, Ohio . . . .
Pennsylvania State University, University Park, Pennsylvania . . . .
Rutgers—The State University, New Brunswick, New Jersey . . . . .
St. Louis University, St. Louis, Missouri . . . .
Southern Illinois University, Carbondale, Illinois . . . .
Stanford University, Stanford, California . . . .
State University of New York—College of Education, Albany, New York . . . .
Tulane University, New Orleans, Louisiana . . . .
University of California, Los Angeles, California . . . .
University of Michigan, Ann Arbor, Michigan . . . .
University of Nevada, Reno, Nevada . . . .
University of Pittsburgh, Pittsburgh, Pennsylvania . . . .
University of Texas, Austin, Texas . . . .
University of Washington, Seattle, Washington . . . .
University of Wisconsin, Madison, Wisconsin . . . .

Faculty Leaders for the Planning Institute, 1961:
Literature—Helen C. White, University of Wisconsin
Language—W. Nelson Francis, Brown University
Composition—Albert Kitzhaber, University of Oregon

Institute Directors	Institute Instructors		
	Literature	Language	Composition
. . . . . . Baxter Hathaway	Ruth Fisher*	Baxter Hathaway	Jonathan Bishop
. . . . . George Williams	Grover Smith	Holger Nygard	George Williams
. . . . . Michael Shinagel	Harold C. Martin	Priscilla Tyler	Scott Elledge*
. . . . . William Wiatt	Terence Martin	Thomas Wetmore*	William Wiatt
. . . . . Walker Gibson	Louise Rosenblatt	Louise Higgins*	Walker Gibson
. . . . . Edwin Robbins	A. E. Wallace Maurer	Leonard Newmark	Edwin Robbins
. . . . . John Bowman	Wilfred T. Jewkes	Agnes McElwee	John Bowman
. . . . . Fred Main	Fred Main	Margaret Bryant*	John A. Myers Jr.*
. . . . . Elias Chiasson	Martin Parry*	J. J. Lamberts*	Elias Chiasson
. . . . . Betty Mitchell	Georgia Winn	Roy Pickett	Fred Lingle
. . . . . Lawrence Ryan	Lawrence Ryan	Robert Ackerman	Craig Vittetoe*
. . . . . David Martin	Carl Niemeyer*	Gretchen Paulus	William Kraus
. . . . . Marvin Morillo	Marvin Morillo	James Downer*	Philip Bollier
. . . . . Charles Hartung	Fred Marcus*	Charles Hartung	R. T. Lenaghan*
. . . . . Arthur Carr	Arthur Carr	Louis C. Rus*	Carlton Wells
. . . . . Jennings Woods	James R. Dickinson	Richard Beal*	John Morrison
. . . . . Dorothy Miller	Dorothy Miller	Alan Markman	Virginia Elliott*
. . . . . W. O. S. Sutherland Jr.	Joseph Slate	David DeCamp	Arnold Lazarus
. . . . . William Irmscher	Edward Bostetter	Donald Emery	Richard Lander*
. . . . . Ednah Thomas	G. Thomas Tanselle	Frederic Cassidy	Ednah Thomas

*Indicates extramural appointment.

Affiliations of Teachers
Who Held Extramural Appointments

Richard Beal . . . . Boston University

Margaret Bryant . . . Brooklyn College

James Downer . . . University of Michigan

Scott Elledge . . . . Cornell University

Virginia Elliott . . . Mount Lebanon High School, Pittsburgh, Pennsylvania

Ruth Fisher . . . . University of Buffalo

Louise Higgins . . . Westport, Connecticut, Public Schools

J. J. Lamberts . . . . Arizona State College

Richard Lander . . . Shoreline High School, Seattle, Washington

R. T. Lenaghan . . . University of Michigan

Fred Marcus . . . . Los Angeles State Teachers' College

John A. Myers Jr. . . The Hun School, Princeton, New Jersey

Carl Niemeyer . . . Union College

Martin Parry . . . . John Burroughs School, St. Louis, Missouri

Louis C. Rus . . . . Calvin College

Craig Vittetoe . . . Palo Alto High School, California

Thomas Wetmore . . Ball State Teachers' College

Second Planning Institute, 1963

Participants	*Schools*	*Addresses*
Mrs. Eleanor Baker . . .	Marshfield Senior High School	Coos Bay, Oregon
Mrs. Eileen McG. Bennett .	Roslyn High School	Roslyn Heights, New York
Miss Ruth E. Bertsch . . .	North Central High School	Indianapolis, Indiana
Mrs. Katherine K. Blunt . .	Ernest W. Seaholm High School	Birmingham, Michigan
Lowell J. Boberg	Jordan High School	Sandy, Utah
Howe Derbyshire	The Cambridge School of Weston	Weston, Massachusetts
Robert G. Donaldson . . .	Denby High School	Detroit, Michigan
Mrs. Prudence O. Dyer . .	James A. Garfield High School	Garrettsville, Ohio
Miss Marion E. Elliott . .	Ithaca High School	Ithaca, New York
Mrs. Martha A. Fisher . .	East Junior High School	Waynesboro, Pennsylvania
Mrs. Mildred Fredericksen .	Webster Groves High School	Webster Groves, Missouri
Conrad D. Geller	Nashoba Regional High School	Bolton, Massachusetts
Richard F. Gregory . . .	Shady Side Academy	Pittsburgh, Pennsylvania
Leroy D. Haley	University Lake School	Hartland, Wisconsin
Michael F. M. Harada . . .	Eagle Rock High School	Los Angeles, California
Mrs. Zelma Boyd Hardy . .	Schreiner Institute	Kerrville, Texas
Seymour C. Heck	Weequahic High School	Newark, New Jersey
William James Hoetker . .	Clayton High School	Clayton, Missouri
Mrs. Gail B. Little	Louise S. McGehee School	New Orleans, Louisiana
Bruce L. MacDonald . . .	Rincon High School	Tucson, Arizona

Participants	Schools	Addresses
Lachlan MacDonald	The Webb School of California	Pomona, California
Mrs. Florence A. Miller	Pierce Junior High School	Grosse Pointe, Michigan
Paul J. McCormick	Hunterdon Central High School	Flemington, New Jersey
Mrs. Joan P. Newman	State Department of Public Instruction	Raleigh, North Carolina
Mrs. Shiho S. Nunes	State Department of Public Instruction	Honolulu, Hawaii
William J. Reynolds	Bellport High School	Bellport, New York
Robert H. Ruebman	Albany High School	Albany, California
James Sabol	Shoreline High School	Seattle, Washington
Ollie Webb Salmon	Columbus Senior High School	Columbus, Indiana
Mrs. Jeanne M. Shaw	Fuquay Springs School	Fuquay Springs, North Carolina
Sister Rita Catherine Hommrich, SCN	Academy of Our Lady of Nazareth	Wakefield, Massachusetts
Mrs. Patricia Smeltzer	Technical High School	Oakland, California
John M. Stewart	Pasadena High School	Pasadena, California
John F. Sutton	Mather Junior High School	Darien, Connecticut
Brother Benedict Torres	Central District Catholic High School	Pittsburgh, Pennsylvania

Participants	Schools	Addresses
Brother George A. Wead, S.M.	Maryhurst Preparatory School	Kirkwood, Missouri
Miss Virginia M. Weis	Our Lady of Mercy High School	Rochester, New York
Robert W. Wheeler	Huron High School	New Boston, Michigan
Mrs. Esther L. H. Williams	Wilmington Senior High School	Wilmington, Ohio
Peter N. Youmans	Pascack Valley Regional High School	Hillsdale, New Jersey

Institute Director, Warner G. Rice
Assistant Director, Arthur Carr

Faculty Leaders:
Language—
 Richard Beal, Boston University
 Miss Louise Higgins, Westport, Connecticut, Public Schools
Literature—
 Wilfred T. Jewkes, The Pennsylvania State University
 Fred Main, Rutgers—The State University
Composition—
 Jonathan Bishop, Cornell University
 William Wiatt, Indiana University

Appendix C.
Commission Kinescopes
and Publications

Kinescopes

To demonstrate tested classroom practices, the Commission on English has undertaken a series of kinescopes addressed to teachers of English in secondary schools and colleges. Copies of these 30-minute representations are available for 16mm motion-picture projection and television. They are widely used in department meetings, conferences, and teacher-training courses. There is no charge other than the costs of shipping. Because of the great demand for these kinescopes, as many as 60 copies of a single film circulate at one time.

Eleven kinescopes are now available:

Teaching a Poem

Leonard Wolf, San Francisco State College

Wolf discusses Shakespeare's "Sonnet 73" as he teaches it to his classes. The Commission does not expect that every teacher will teach each sonnet in this fashion. It believes, however, that Wolf's approach is exciting and provocative, a brilliant example of how one man teaches a poem.

A Student Writing Assignment Based on "Fire Walking in Ceylon"

Arthur Carr, University of Michigan

Drawing on his own experience, Carr demonstrates the proper adjustment of form and idea in making a student writing assignment. The Commission thinks that even the most experienced teacher will derive practical benefits from his explanation.

A Class Study of Theodore Roethke's "The Waking"

Alice C. Coleman, Mission Bay High School, San Diego, California

Mrs. Coleman describes how she teaches Theodore Roethke's "The Waking" to a high school class. Careful and intelligent planning, she shows, can keep students in close study of the structure and the literal meaning of a poem and hold in check students' efforts to suggest prematurely what the poet "means."

162

Teaching Biography in the Secondary School

    Darcy Curwen, Phillips Exeter Academy

    With particular reference to Boswell's *Life of Johnson,* Curwen shows the unique rewards, for teachers and for students, in the study of literary biography. Other works discussed by Curwen are Moss Hart's *Act I,* W. Somerset Maugham's *The Summing Up,* and Catherine Drinker Bowen's *Yankee from Olympus.*

Teaching Shakespeare's "Henry IV, Part I"

    Hallett Smith, California Institute of Technology

    Smith recommends the study of *Henry IV, Part I* in secondary schools. He considers the different kinds of language and their uses, studies the narrative and dramatic structure, and finds the great themes of the play presented directly in powerful poetic and comic language. Viewers will share his enthusiasm for this play and like his helpful suggestions.

Grammar and Generative Grammar

    Karl V. Teeter, Harvard University

    Teeter shows how "generative grammar" takes off from a theory of the nature of all languages and demonstrates how the terms of that theory are realized and related for a particular language. This film will give teachers some notion of what makes language tick.

The "Speaking Voice" and the Teaching of Composition

    Walker Gibson, New York University

    Through "role" and "voice," Gibson explores an old, but ever new, method of defining ourselves in composition. He uses several pieces of literature to assist teachers in recognizing the huge implications of "the speaking voice."

Invention and Topics: or, Where to Look for Something to Say

    Scott Elledge, Cornell University

    Elledge, relating Aristotle's theory of rhetoric to composition, makes clear that a good composition assignment gives a student something to

163

make a discovery about. The kinescope is a strong affirmation that invention and arrangement are properly part of the art of rhetoric.

Organization—Rhetorical and Artistic

George Williams, Duke University

Williams uses the vitality and subtlety of Bernard DeVoto's essay "Seed Corn and Mistletoe" to demonstrate that the basis for coherence and wholeness in writing is lodged in the writer's understanding of order and logic.

Teaching a Short Story: Faulkner's "Barn Burning"

Sarah Youngblood, University of Minnesota

Using narrative, plot, setting, and characters as the basis for her discussion, Miss Youngblood makes clear that the originality of an author lies not so much in the subject he treats as in the way he treats it. The vocabulary and method used in explaining "Barn Burning" will be useful to teachers in examining any story.

Teaching a Novel: "Moby Dick" in the Classroom

Terence Martin, Indiana University

Martin attempts to unify the major forces in *Moby Dick*—Ahab, the whale, and the sea—with the large meaning of theme in the novel. Teachers will also find in considerable detail a useful discussion of symbol, language, form, and point of view.

Other kinescopes are planned for production in the near future.

Requests to use kinescopes should be in writing. Please make reservations, whenever possible, at least two months in advance of planned showing. This will nearly always insure that the films will be available when you need them. The mailing cost from the Commission's film service in Watertown—library rate and special delivery—is 78 cents for one film, 98 cents for two in a single shipment.

All correspondence (letters, checks, money orders, and so forth) concerning kinescopes should be addressed to Commission on English,

687 Boylston Street, Boston, Massachusetts 02116. If possible, and in order to save billing by the Commission office, please enclose shipping charges in the correct amount with your order.

Note: Immediately after showing, kinescopes should be returned to Cine Service Laboratories, Inc., 51 Kondazian Street, Watertown, Massachusetts 02172, special delivery, at the postal rate for library materials.

Publications

End-of-Year Examinations in English for College-Bound Students, Grades 9-12

The purpose of this book is to define for English teachers—in precise, practical, and helpful terms—some of the skills and understandings the Commission believes a college preparatory student ought to have acquired by the end of each year of secondary school, grades 9-12.

The book consists basically of four examinations designed for the end of grades 9, 10, 11, and 12. Each examination has three questions: one in language, literature, and composition; and each examination question is followed by actual student answers, ranging from excellent to poor, with detailed analysis and evaluation of each answer. Supplementary questions and commentary on student reactions to them provide further illustrations of the Commission's objectives.

The Commission chose this method of reporting its recommendations at the very outset of its attempts to specify, first for itself and then for the entire educational community, what English is and what it ought to be. The members of the Commission knew from experience that a teacher defines most sharply and revealingly what he believes about English in the examination questions he sets for his students.

The project began in 1960 with the preparation of an experimental end-of-year twelfth-grade examination which was tried out on 1,200 college freshmen. When the enthusiastic responses of teachers to the resulting report showed that similar materials for the earlier secondary school grades would be of great practical value to teachers throughout the country, examination questions were prepared for grades 9, 10, and 11. The questions that appear in the book were selected for their effectiveness in trials in 27 secondary schools. The student answers that accompany each question were obtained by administering the examinations in 25 additional schools in May 1962.

Copies of this volume, now in its second printing, may be ordered from the College Entrance Examination Board, Publications Order Office, Box 592, Princeton, New Jersey 08540; or Box 1025, Berkeley, California 94701. The price is $2 per copy.

Publications Now Out of Print

The following documents, which were useful to show the Commission's changing point of view, are now out of print: *The Summer Institute Program—An Interim Report of the Commission on English—February 1962; A Progress Report for 1959-63; Preparation in English for College-Bound Students; Summer Institutes for English Teachers.*

Summer Institute Materials

With the extension of the National Defense Education Act, October 1964, to include English in the National Defense Institutes for Advanced Studies, the Modern Language Association offered to publish Commission on English materials concerned with Summer Institutes. Through the Modern Language Association, one can purchase the following:

College Preparation in English. A working paper of the Commission on English giving the rationale for the 1962 Summer English Institutes. 8 pages. 25 cents. MLA Code W11.

The Evaluation of the 1962 Summer English Institutes. By John C. Gerber. 75 pages. $1. MLA Code W12.

The 1962 Summer Institutes of the Commission on English: Their Achievement and Promise. By John C. Gerber. *PMLA,* September 1963. An abridgement of W12. 19 pages. 25 cents. MLA Code W13.

The Commission on English 1962 Summer Institutes for English Teachers. A packet of 11 items detailing the background of the 1962 Summer Institutes, their syllabi and bibliographies for courses in language, literature, and composition, extracts from institute directors' reports, workshops, and the follow-up program. 125 pages. $2. MLA Code W14.

Address orders and correspondence concerning orders to: Publications Section, Modern Language Association, 4 Washington Place, New York, New York 10003.

Appendix D.
Bibliographies

The three bibliographies that follow list books an English teacher should ideally have within easy reach, either in his home library, his classroom, or his departmental library. For none of the categories are all the useful books named, but for some more than one is mentioned, discrimination among the alternatives following in a brief note. Some valuable standard works have gone out of print (Henry Sweet's *Grammar,* for instance) and are not mentioned (even though secondhand copies might be located after industrious search), unless nothing else of comparable merit or usefulness is now available directly from publishers. If a book is out of print, a notation is made at the end of the entry. Paperback editions currently available are noted. (Warning: many paperback reprints are "retired" by their publisher after a single issue if sales are not brisk. For that reason, some paperback editions may not be available when this list appears even though it has been checked as close as possible to the time of publication.)

Language

Bloomfield, Leonard. *Language.* New York: Henry Holt and Company [Holt, Rinehart and Winston, Inc.], 1933.

Jespersen, Otto. *Language: Its Nature, Development, and Origin.* London: G. Allen and Unwin, Ltd., 1922. Paperback: W. W. Norton & Co., Inc.

Sapir, Edward. *Language: An Introduction to the Study of Speech.* New York: Harcourt, Brace and Company [Harcourt, Brace & World, Inc.], 1921. Paperback: Harvest Books.

Despite similarity in title, these books are distinctly different in point of view. Sapir is speculative and discursive and deals with theory of language. Jespersen is philological and historical. Bloomfield adds analytic concerns, especially with sounds; his book is the basis for later "structural" study of language.

Jespersen, Otto. *Essentials of English Grammar.* New York: Henry Holt and Company [Holt, Rinehart and Winston, Inc.], 1933; University, Ala.: University of Alabama Press, 1964.

Long, Ralph. *The Sentence and Its Parts.* Chicago: The University of Chicago Press, 1961.

Both works are "scholarly traditional." Jespersen's one volume is only the essence of his seven-volume study, which remains a storehouse of reference. Long brings traditional grammar up to date, in the light of mid-twentieth-century English and English studies.

Allen, Harold B. (ed.). *Readings in Applied English Linguistics.* New York: Appleton-Century-Crofts, Inc., 1958. *Second edition:* 1964. Paperback only.

Francis, W. Nelson. *The Structure of American English.* New York: The Ronald Press Co., 1958.

Fries, Charles C. *The Structure of English: An Introduction to the Construction of English Sentences.* New York: Harcourt, Brace and Company [Harcourt, Brace & World, Inc.], 1952.

Gleason, H. A., Jr. *An Introduction to Descriptive Linguistics.* New York: Henry Holt and Company, 1955. *Second edition:* New York: Holt, Rinehart and Winston, Inc., 1961.

Sledd, James. *A Short Introduction to English Grammar.* Chicago: Scott, Foresman and Company, 1959.

Fries's text is the cornerstone of structural grammar. Gleason gives a general survey of this school of linguists. Francis' work is a very succinct structural grammar containing a chapter on practical application ("Linguistics and the Teacher of English"). The Francis book also contains an exceptionally fine chapter on American English dialects by Raven I. McDavid Jr. Sledd provides a reconciliation between traditional and structural grammar. The Allen anthology surveys practical implications of structural studies. The 1964 edition also includes articles on transformational grammar.

Chomsky, Noam. *Syntactic Structures.* The Hague: Mouton & Co., 1957. Paperback: Humanities Press.

Fodor, J. A., and J. J. Katz (eds.). *The Structure of Language: Readings in the Philosophy of Language.* Englewood Cliffs, N. J.: Prentice-Hall, Inc., 1964.

Roberts, Paul. *English Syntax.* New York: Harcourt, Brace & World, Inc., 1964. Paperback only.

Rogovin, Syrell. *Modern English Sentence Structure.* New York: Random House, Inc., 1964.

Chomsky's monograph is the basis for transformational studies. Roberts' text is programed for the high school student and Rogovin's for the junior high school student. The Fodor and Katz anthology contains significant and some otherwise inaccessible papers on language theory, grammar, semantics, and psychological implications.

Baugh, Albert C. *A History of the English Language.* New York: D. Appleton Century Co., Inc., 1935. *Second edition:* New York: Appleton-Century-Crofts, Inc., 1957.

Mencken, H. L. *The American Language.* New York: Alfred A. Knopf, Inc., 1919. *Second edition:* 1921. *Third edition:* 1923. *Fourth edition* (including the two supplements), abridged by Raven I. McDavid Jr.: 1963.

Pyles, Thomas. *The Origins and Development of the English Language.* New York: Harcourt, Brace & World, Inc., 1964.

Baugh's book is strong in details of external history: the social, political, and intellectual forces that have affected the growth of English. Using all the tools of contemporary linguistics, Pyles stresses the internal history of the language: the phonological and grammatical development of American and British English. His linguistic analysis of Shakespeare's English should be especially useful to classroom teachers. Mencken's work, the first attempt at a history of American English, remains rich in illustration and stimulation.

Bryant, Margaret M. (ed.). *Current American Usage.* New York: Funk & Wagnalls Company, Inc., 1962.

Gove, Philip B., and others (eds.). *Webster's Third New International Dictionary.* Springfield, Mass.: G. & C. Merriam Company, 1961.

Kurath, Hans, and Raven I. McDavid Jr. *The Pronunciation of English in the Atlantic States.* Ann Arbor, Mich.: The University of Michigan Press, 1961.

Mathews, Mitford McL. (ed.). *A Dictionary of Americanisms on Historical Principles.* Chicago: The University of Chicago Press, 1951.

Murray, J. A. H. (ed.). *Oxford English Dictionary.* London: Oxford University Press, 1933, 13 volumes.

These books should help the teacher who wants to make a serious inquiry into the nature of error and correctness, who wants to be able to substantiate his red-pencil strictures. The Oxford aims to report meaning, origin, and history of all English words used or known to have been used from the Middle English period to its publication date. It remains the most scholarly dictionary of the language. Webster, the only American unabridged dictionary, represents the most recent authoritative but not authoritarian report on usage. The *Dictionary of Americanisms* reports on words and expressions that originated in the United States, whether as neologisms, loan words, or new usages of British English. Kurath's work with linguistic atlases gives reliable information about pronunciation, dialects, and usage. The Bryant book is very comprehensive; it takes the long view of usage variants.

Literature

Critical Histories (Comprehensive)

Trent, W. P., and others (eds.). *Cambridge History of American Literature.* Cambridge, England: Cambridge University Press, 1917-1921, 4 volumes. New York: The Macmillan Company, 1943, 1 volume.

Ward, A. W., and A. R. Waller (eds.). *Cambridge History of English Literature.* Cambridge, England: Cambridge University Press, 1907-1916, 14 volumes. *General Index,* 1927, Volume 15.

These are the basic multivolume critical histories. In both, specialists have been called on for the various periods, movements, and literary forms. Though both sets were completed decades ago and therefore cannot reflect historical, critical, and linguistic study of later date, they remain rich depositories of information and judgment.

Baugh, Albert C., and others. *A Literary History of England.* New York: Appleton-Century-Crofts, Inc. (text edition); Des Moines: Meredith Press (trade edition).

Spiller, Robert E., and others. *Literary History of the United States.* New York: The Macmillan Company, 1948, 3 volumes. *Revised edition:* 1953, 1 volume.

These extensive, one-volume studies, each the work of several scholars, and both much more recent than the Cambridge histories, are the standard works of their kind.

Critical Histories (English, by Period)

Ker, William P. *English Literature: Medieval.* New York: Henry Holt and Company [Holt, Rinehart & Winston, Inc.], 1912.

Schlauch, Margaret. *English Medieval Literature and Its Social Foundations.* Cambridge, England: W. Heffer and Sons, Ltd., 1956.

Ker's book is short and uncomplicated and has been for half a century the book for initiation to the field. Schlauch's book is more comprehensive and more detailed (includes Old English, Latin, Anglo-French, and Vernacular literature).

Chute, Marchette. *Geoffrey Chaucer of England*. New York: E. P. Dutton & Co.,
   Inc., 1946. Paperback: Everyman Paperbacks.
An unspecialized but sound combination of biography, social history, and literary
criticism, this study has the additional merit of being very readable.

Granville-Barker, Harley. *Prefaces to Shakespeare*. Princeton, N. J.: Princeton
   University Press, 1946, Volume 1; 1947, Volume 2.
Harbage, Alfred. *William Shakespeare: A Reader's Guide*. New York: Farrar,
   Straus & Co., Inc., 1963. Paperback: The Noonday Press.
Granville-Barker's famous "Prefaces," originally lectures, have been revised and
reprinted in this Princeton edition. Harbage's recent book is an ingenious
"progress" through the plays, bringing broad scholarship and sound critical
commentary to particular passages.

Of the many complete editions of Shakespeare's plays, several are heavily
enough annotated to be of much help to a teacher. It is now again possible,
moreover, to acquire copies of the *Furness Variorum* which is being reissued
in inexpensive paperback format by Dover Publications, Inc. Of the many
annotated, one-play-a-volume texts, the Arden editions may come closest to
serving both the scholarly teacher and the good secondary school student.

Bush, Douglas. *English Literature in the Earlier Seventeenth Century, 1600-
   1660. The Oxford History of English Literature, Volume 5*. London: The
   Clarendon Press, 1945. *Revised edition:* London: Oxford University Press,
   1962.
Willey, Basil. *The Seventeenth Century Background: Studies in the Thought
   of the Age in Relation to Poetry and Religion*. London: Chatto & Windus,
   1934; New York: Columbia University Press, 1942. Paperback: Anchor
   Books.
These two books provide a valuable supplement to the general histories, Willey's
for its overview of the entire intellectual scene, Bush's for its discerning and
lucid literary criticism.

Nicolson, Harold G. *The Age of Reason, 1700-1789*. London: Constable & Co.,
   Ltd., 1960; New York: Doubleday & Co., Inc., 1961 [in U. S. titled *The Age
   of Reason; the 18th Century*].
This volume is clear, thorough, and judicious.

Hough, Graham G. *The Romantic Poets*. London: Hutchinson & Co. (Publishers) Ltd. Hutchinson's University Library, 1953. Paperback: W. W. Norton & Co., Inc.

Jack, Ian. *English Literature, 1815-1832. Oxford History of English Literature, Volume X.* London: Oxford University Press, 1963.

The compass of Hough's book is the smaller of these two, but its criticism is very discerning. Jack's is a substantial study.

Holloway, John. *The Victorian Sage: Studies in Argument.* London: Macmillan & Co., Ltd., 1953.

Houghton, Walter E. *The Victorian Frame of Mind, 1830-1870.* New Haven, Conn.: Yale University Press, 1957. Hard cover or paperback.

The first of these two books is an engaging study of the major Victorian prose writers; the second is an exploration of attitudes, concepts, premises, and preoccupations.

No book dealing with all the major Victorian poets presents substantially richer fare than is available in the relevant sections of Baugh's *Literary History* or of the *Cambridge History of English Literature.*

Critical Histories (American, by Period)

Miller, Perry G. E. *The New England Mind: The Seventeenth Century.* Cambridge, Mass.: Harvard University Press, 1954. Paperback: Beacon Press.

Parrington, Vernon Louis. *Main Currents in American Thought: An Interpretation of American Literature from the Beginnings to 1920.* New York: Harcourt, Brace and Company [Harcourt, Brace & World, Inc.], 1927-1930, 3 volumes. 1939, 1 volume. Paperback: Harvest Books.

These two studies are important background matter for the teacher. Neither is exclusively or even primarily literary in emphasis: Miller's emphasizes the intellectual (especially the religious) forces at work in the development of our national literature, and Parrington's emphasizes the social forces.

Cowie, Alexander. *The Rise of the American Novel.* New York: American Book Company, 1948. Out of print.

Pearce, Roy Harvey. *The Continuity of American Poetry.* Princeton, N. J.: Princeton University Press, 1961.

Quinn, Arthur H. *A History of the American Drama from the Civil War to the Present Day.* New York: Harper and Brothers [Harper & Row, Publishers, Inc.], 1927. *Second edition:* New York: Appleton-Century-Crofts, 1943.

Of several one-volume histories of American fiction, Cowie's is the most generally satisfactory, though that by Edward Wagenknecht (*Cavalcade of the American Novel*. New York: Henry Holt and Company, 1952) is both sound and thorough and will serve teachers' needs about as well. Quinn's book is without peer. Pearce's is the only recent attempt to bring American poetry, from Anne Bradstreet to Wallace Stevens, into one frame.

Brooks, Van Wyck. *New England: Indian Summer, 1865-1915.* New York: E. P. Dutton & Company, Inc., 1940. Out of print.

Kazin, Alfred. *On Native Grounds: An Interpretation of Modern American Prose Literature.* New York: Reynal & Hitchcock, 1942. Now published by Harcourt, Brace & World, Inc.

Lawrence, D. H. *Studies in Classic American Literature.* New York: Thomas Seltzer, Inc., 1923. Paperback: Compass Books.

Matthiessen, Francis O. *American Renaissance: Art and Expression in the Age of Emerson and Whitman.* New York: Oxford University Press, 1941.

Smith, Henry Nash. *Virgin Land: The American West as Symbol and Myth.* Cambridge, Mass.: Harvard University Press, 1950. Paperback: Vintage Books.

Wilson, Edmund. *Classics and Commercials: A Literary Chronicle of the Forties.* New York: Farrar, Straus & Young, Inc. [Farrar, Straus & Giroux, Inc.], 1950. Paperback: Vintage Books.

Winters, Yvor. *Maule's Curse: Seven Studies in the History of American Obscurantism.* Norfolk, Conn.: New Directions, 1938. Out of print.

These are but a few of the general studies, more critical than historical, that have established themselves as seminal inquiries, valuable for their penetration or for their vigorously argued judgments or for attention to writers and works less important for quality than for influence.

Modern Studies in Theory and Genre

Burke, Kenneth. *The Philosophy of Literary Form: Studies in Symbolic Action.* Baton Rouge, La.: Louisiana State University Press, 1941. Paperback: Vintage Books.

Crane, Ronald S. *The Languages of Criticism and the Structure of Poetry.* Toronto: University of Toronto Press, 1953. Hard cover and paperback.

Frye, Northrop. *The Anatomy of Criticism; Four Essays.* Princeton, N. J.: Princeton University Press, 1957.

Richards, I. A. *Practical Criticism: A Study of Literary Judgment.* London: K. Paul, Trench, Trubner and Company, 1929. Paperback: Harvest Books.

Fergusson, Francis. *The Human Image in Dramatic Literature.* Gloucester, Mass.: Peter Smith, 1957 (the Anchor Books edition bound in cloth). Paperback: Anchor Books.

Lucas, F. L. *Tragedy: Serious Drama in Relation to Aristotle's "Poetics."* New York: Harcourt, Brace and Company [Harcourt, Brace & World, Inc.], 1928. Paperback: Collier Books.

Nicoll, Allardyce. *The Theory of Drama.* London: G. G. Harrap and Company, 1931; New York: Thomas Y. Crowell Company, 1931. Out of print.

Ker, William P. *Epic and Romance: Essays on Medieval Literature.* London: Macmillan and Company, Ltd.; New York: The Macmillan Company, 1897; Gloucester, Mass.: Peter Smith, 1963 (the Dover Publications edition bound in cloth). Paperback: Dover Publications, Inc.

Booth, Wayne. *The Rhetoric of Fiction.* Chicago, Ill.: The University of Chicago Press, 1961. Hard cover and paperback.

Brower, Reuben A. *The Fields of Light: An Experiment in Critical Reading.* New York: Oxford University Press, 1951. Paperback: Galaxy Books.

Drew, Elizabeth. *The Modern Novel: Some Aspects of Contemporary Fiction.* New York: Harcourt, Brace and Company [Harcourt, Brace & World, Inc.], 1926. Out of print.

Forster, E. M. *Aspects of the Novel.* New York: Harcourt, Brace and Company [Harcourt, Brace & World, Inc.], 1927. Paperback: Harvest Books.

Lubbock, Percy. *The Craft of Fiction.* London: Jonathan Cape, 1921; New York: Jonathan Cape and Harrison Smith, 1929. *New edition:* New York: The Viking Press, 1957. Paperback: Compass Books.

Van Ghent, Dorothy. *The English Novel: Form and Function.* New York: Rinehart & Company, Inc. [Holt, Rinehart and Winston, Inc.], 1953. Paperback: Torchbooks.

Blackmur, R. P. *The Double Agent: Essays in Craft and Elucidation.* New York: Arrow Editions Co-operative Association, Inc., 1935 (out of print); Gloucester, Mass.: Peter Smith, 1962.

Brooks, Cleanth, and Robert Penn Warren (eds.). *Understanding Poetry: An Anthology for College Students.* New York: Henry Holt and Company, 1938. *Revised edition:* New York: Holt, Rinehart and Winston, Inc., 1960.

Deutsch, Babette. *Poetry in Our Time.* New York: Henry Holt and Company [Holt, Rinehart and Winston, Inc.], 1952. Paperback: Anchor Books (second revised edition, 1963).

Gregory, Horace. *The Shield of Achilles: Essays on Beliefs in Poetry.* New York: Harcourt, Brace and Company [Harcourt, Brace & World, Inc.], 1944. Out of print.

Miles, Josephine. *Eras and Modes in English Poetry. Second revised edition:* Berkeley, Calif.: University of California Press, 1964. Paperback: University of California Press (second edition, revised and enlarged).

Ransom, John Crowe. *The World's Body.* New York: Charles Scribner's Sons, 1938 (out of print). Now published by Kennikat Press, Port Washington, N.Y.

Rosenthal, M. L., and A. J. M. Smith. *Exploring Poetry.* New York: The Macmillan Company, 1955.

Winters, Yvor. *Anatomy of Nonsense.* Norfolk, Conn.: New Directions, 1943.

Composition

Aristotle.
  Rhetoric.
  Topics.
  Posterior Analytics.
  Sophistical Elenches.
Cicero.
  Of Invention.
  Topics.
  Of the Orator.
Plato.
  Phaedrus.
Quintillian.
  Oratorical Institutes.

These are the classical works from which, in one way or another, all formal rhetorical study until modern times takes its start. The two Greek authors make hard reading (especially Aristotle), but some knowledge of both is desirable. Cicero and Quintillian are more practical than theoretical, but "practice" with them is far from casual.

Burke, Kenneth. *A Philosophy of Literary Form.* Baton Rouge, La.: University of Louisiana Press, 1941. Paperback: Vintage Books (revised edition, 1957).

Fogarty, Daniel. *Roots for a New Rhetoric.* New York: Bureau of Publications, Teachers College, Columbia University, 1959. Out of print.

Hayakawa, Samuel I. *Language in Thought and Action.* New York: Harcourt, Brace and Company [Harcourt, Brace & World, Inc.], 1949. (Based on *Language in Action,* 1939). Paperback: Harvest Books.

Richards, I. A. *Philosophy of Rhetoric.* New York and London: Oxford University Press, 1936.

Shannon, Claude E., and Warren Weaver. *Mathematical Theory of Communication.* Urbana, Ill.: University of Illinois Press, 1949. Paperback: Insight Books.

Father Fogarty's short study analyzes some of the changed conditions and attitudes that make a new rhetoric necessary. The other books named in this group illustrate attempts to formulate a modern rhetoric from different bases: sociological (Burke), psychological (Hayakawa), semantic (Richards), and communications (Shannon and Weaver).

Boulton, Marjorie. *The Anatomy of Prose.* London: Routledge and Paul, Ltd., 1954; New York: Hillary House Pubs., Ltd.

Brooks, Cleanth, and Robert Penn Warren. *Modern Rhetoric.* New York: Harcourt, Brace and Company, 1949. Paperback: Harcourt, Brace & World, Inc.

Chittick, Roger D., and Robert D. Stevick. *Rhetoric for Exposition.* New York: Appleton-Century-Crofts, 1961.

Graves, Robert, and Alan Hodge. *Reader Over Your Shoulder.* New York: The Macmillan Company, 1943. Hard cover and paperback.

Martin, Harold C. *Logic and Rhetoric of Exposition.* New York: Rinehart & Company, Inc., 1958. *Revised edition:* With Richard M. Ohmann. New York: Holt, Rinehart and Winston, Inc., 1963.

School and college rhetoric textbooks are legion. Those listed above are attempts to approach writing problems single-mindedly, and each is enough different from any other in the group to provide a spectrum of texts beyond the "handbook" kind.

Beach, Joseph Warren. *The Outlook for American Prose.* Chicago: The University of Chicago Press, 1926. Out of print.

Dobrée, Bonamy. *Modern Prose Style.* London: The Clarendon Press, 1934. *Second edition:* 1964.

Murry, J. M. *The Problem of Style.* London and New York: Oxford University Press, 1922. Paperback: New York: Oxford University Press, 1960.

Read, Herbert. *English Prose Style.* London: G. Bell and Sons, Ltd., 1928. *Revised edition:* Bell & Sons, Ltd., 1952. Paperback: Beacon Press.
Williams, William Carlos. *In the American Grain.* Norfolk, Conn.: New Directions, 1939. Paperback only.
All these books are addressed in interesting ways to general problems of prose style. Murry's book derives from a famous French work by Rémy de Gourmont. Read's represents a serious effort to take account of changes in style stemming from new psychological attitudes and understandings. Of the other three, that by the poet William Carlos Williams is the most provocative, but both of the others repay study.

This book was designed by Freeman Craw. It was composed in the Garamond types by Tri-Arts Press, Inc., New York, and printed by offset lithography at New York Lithographing Corp., New York. The cloth edition was bound by Russell-Rutter Co., Inc., New York, and the paper edition by Fisher Bookbinding Co., Inc., New York.